THE HARTLEY AP® WORLD HISTORY STUDY GUIDE 2024

Everything You Need to Know to Ace SAQ, DBQ & LEQ, Get an A in Your Class and Score a 5 on The APWH Exam Day

By
The Hartley Publishing

COPYRIGHT AND DISCLAIMER

Copyright © 2023 by The Hartley Publishing. All rights reserved.

Cover Image: Mirko Kuzmanovic / Shutterstock.com

Without the author's written permission, no part of this study guide may be copied, stored in a retrieval system, or sent in any way, including by photocopying, recording, or any other method.

This study guide is designed to be used as a supplemental resource for students preparing for the Advanced Placement World History Exam. The information and advice contained herein are based on the author's personal experience and research and are intended to provide general guidance to students.

Even though the author has done everything possible to make sure the information in this study guide is correct, he or she is not responsible for any mistakes, omissions, or results that may come from using this information. The author is not responsible for any injuries or damages that come from using or not using this study guide correctly. The author recommends that students consult with their teachers or academic advisors for specific guidance on exam preparation and study strategies.

Furthermore, the author does not guarantee the suitability of the study guide for any particular purpose or individual. Every student is unique and may have different learning styles and needs. Therefore, the author encourages students to use this study guide as a starting point for their exam preparation and customize their approach to fit their learning preferences and academic goals.

The author is not affiliated with the College Board or the Advanced Placement Program, and this study guide is not endorsed by or affiliated with these organizations. The views and opinions in this study guide are those of the person who wrote it, not necessarily those of the College Board or any other group.

The author of this study guide is not responsible for the content or availability of any outside websites or resources that are linked to it. These links are provided for convenience and informational purposes only, and the author does not endorse or guarantee the accuracy, reliability, or appropriateness of any information contained on these sites. Students should use caution when accessing external websites and follow appropriate safety guidelines and practices.

By using this study guide, you agree to the terms and conditions of this Copyright and Disclaimer statement.

TABLE OF CONTENTS

INTRODUCTION 1
EXAM FORMAT AND STRUCTURE 3
  Section I (Multiple Choice and Short Answer) 3
    Part A: Multiple-Choice Questions 3
    Part B: Short-Answer Questions 4
  Section II: Free Response 6
    1. Document-Based Question (DBQ) 6
    2. Long Essay Question (LEQ) 8
STRATEGIES FOR ANSWERING THE MULTIPLE-CHOICE QUESTIONS 11
  1. Employing the Process of Elimination 11
  2. Identify Context Cues 13
  3. Identify Patterns and Themes 19
  4. Time Management and Pacing 21
  Sample Multiple-Choice Questions With Answer 26
  Sample Questions and Model Answers 53
EXCELLING IN THE DBQ (DOCUMENT-BASED QUESTION) 55
  Analyzing Primary Source Documents 55
  Constructing a Strong Thesis Statement 56
  Constructing a Coherent Argument 57
  Sample DBQs and Model Essays 61
TACKLING THE LEQ (LONG ESSAY QUESTION) 66
  How to Successfully Tackle the Long Essay Question (LEQ) in World History 66
  Sample LEQs and Model Essays 70
COMPREHENSIVE CONTENT REVIEW 74
  Unit 1: The Global Tapestry (1200 - 1450) 74
  Unit 2: Networks of Exchange (1200 - 1450) 75
  Unit 3: Land-Based Empires (1450 - 1750) 77

Unit 4: Transoceanic Interconnections (1450 - 1750) *78*
Unit 5: Revolutions (1750 - 1900) *80*
Unit 6: Industrialization's Effects (1750 to 1900) *81*
Unit 7: Worldwide Confrontations (1900 - Present) *83*
Unit 8: Cold War and Decolonization (1945 - 1989) *84*
Unit 9: The Age of Global Interconnectedness (Post-1989 to Now) *85*

EFFECTIVE WAYS TO STUDY AND TOOLS TO USE **88**
1. Creating a Study Plan and Schedule *88*
2. Utilizing Flashcards, Mnemonics, and Other Memory Aids *89*
    a. Flashcards *89*
    b. Mnemonics...*90*
    c. Mind Maps And Timelines *91*
3. Take Advantage of Online Resources and Study Groups..*92*
    a. Online Resources *92*
    b. Study Groups..*93*

TEST DAY STRATEGIES AND TIPS **95**
Prepare Mentally and Physically for the Exam..*95*
Manage Stress and Anxiety *97*
Make the Most of Your Time During the Test *99*

CONCLUSION **102**

RESOURCES AND TOOLS **104**

INTRODUCTION

The Advanced Placement (AP) World History exam is renowned for its rigorous nature, given its comprehensive coverage of extensive historical periods across the globe, spanning thousands of years. Adequately preparing for this examination necessitates a profound comprehension of historical events, concepts, and proficiencies. These include the critical analysis of primary and secondary sources, the formulation of historical arguments, and the interpretation of historical data.

As experienced educators and history enthusiasts, we understand students' challenges when preparing for the AP World History exam. We have developed a carefully curated study guide that is designed to streamline your preparation for the AP World History exam. Our team has dedicated significant effort to create this comprehensive resource, leveraging our expertise in writing and publishing, as well as our deep understanding of the exam. This guide encompasses all the vital information and skills required for success on exam day. Our aim is to simplify the intricate themes and content, empowering you to approach the exam with confidence and achieve the best possible results. This guide is your ultimate companion in mastering AP World History, from test-taking strategies to unit-specific study guides, review materials, and resources.

Using The Hartley AP World History Study Guide 2024, you will benefit from a structured study approach, time-saving strategies, and in-depth explanations of question types and formats. Our practice questions, prompts, and sample essays will help you sharpen your skills and build your confidence. We have also included key terms, a timeline of major events, and primary source documents to enhance your understanding of the historical context.

However, do not rely on our words alone. Our study guide's effectiveness is demonstrated by the achievements of our past students who have utilized our strategies to attain top scores on the AP World History exam. With our guidance, you have the potential to surpass your own expectations and achieve similar levels of success as others before you.

We are confident in making this promise to you: Our study guide will provide you with the essential knowledge, skills, and confidence needed to excel on the AP World History exam, achieve an outstanding grade in your class, and obtain a score of 5 on the APWH exam. We firmly believe that with a great promise comes a great outcome, and we are dedicated to supporting you in achieving the best possible results.

But don't wait – start preparing today! The AP World History exam is just around the corner, and every minute counts. Start using this study guide now to streamline your preparation and boost your chances of success.

So, are you ready to confidently embark on your AP World History journey and achieve your academic goals? Turn the pages of this study guide, and let us guide you toward success. It's time to take charge of your exam preparation and make history with The AP World History Study Guide 2024.

EXAM FORMAT AND STRUCTURE

The Advanced Placement (AP) World History exam is a comprehensive assessment designed to evaluate students' understanding of world history concepts, historical events, and historical analysis skills. The regularly scheduled exam date for the AP World History exam is on Thursday morning, May 11, 2023, with a late-testing exam date on Friday afternoon, May 19, 2023.

Section I (Multiple Choice and Short Answer)
There are two sections in Section I of the AP World History exam:

Part A: Multiple-Choice Questions

Part A of Section I in the AP World History exam consists of Multiple-Choice Questions designed to assess your knowledge and understanding of world history and your ability to analyze historical sources and contexts. In this part, you must answer 55 multiple-choice questions within 55 minutes.

The skills tested in Part A can be broadly categorized as follows:

- **Content Knowledge**

You must demonstrate your understanding of world history's key events, developments, and processes. This includes knowledge of specific civilizations, time periods, regions, and major themes such as political structures, economic systems, social patterns, cultural trends, and technological advancements.

- **Source Analysis**

Primary or secondary sources, such as excerpts from historical texts, images, maps, or charts, will accompany many multiple-choice questions. You must be able to interpret these sources, identify their purpose, point of view, or intended audience, and understand the content and its relation to the question being asked.

- **Comparison and Contextualization**

It is essential to possess the ability to analyze and compare historical advancements across diverse societies, regions, and time periods. Additionally, you should be capable of contextualizing historical events and processes within broader regional, global, or chronological frameworks, showcasing your comprehension of the interconnections within world history.

- **Cause and Effect**

You must recognize and evaluate the relationships between multiple causes and effects, considering both short-term and long-term impacts. This skill involves identifying and analyzing the factors that contribute to historical events or developments and the consequences that result from them.

- **Continuity and Change over Time**

You need to identify and analyze patterns of change and continuity throughout history. You should be able to recognize how societies and institutions have evolved or remained consistent across time and understand the factors that drive these transformations or maintain stability.

During the multiple-choice section, each question presents only one correct answer. The final score will be determined by the number of correct responses provided.

Part B: Short-Answer Questions

Part B of Section I in the AP World History Exam consists of Short-Answer Questions (SAQs). This section assesses your ability to provide specific examples, explanations, or analyses in response to a given historical prompt. Within the allocated 40-minute time limit, you will need to respond to three short-answer questions. The first two questions are mandatory, indicating that you must provide answers for them. As for the third question, you have the flexibility to select between two alternatives (Question 3 or Question 4) and answer the one of your choosing.

The skills tested in Part B can be broadly categorized as follows:

- **Developing Arguments**

You must be able to develop a thesis or claim that addresses the question. This skill involves crafting clear, concise, and well-organized responses that present a coherent argument supported by historical evidence.

- **Using Specific Historical Examples**

You need to provide relevant examples to support your arguments, demonstrating a thorough understanding of historical events, processes, or developments. This skill requires you to recall and apply specific details, facts, and concepts from your study of world history.

- **Analyzing Cause and Effect**

Similar to Part A, it is essential to recognize and assess the connections between multiple causes and effects in your responses. This encompasses the consideration of both immediate and long-lasting effects. It is important to be able to recognize and evaluate the multiple factors influencing historical events or progressions, as well as the subsequent outcomes that arise from them.

- **Comparison and Contextualization**

You are expected to possess the ability to compare historical advancements across various societies, regions, and time periods. Additionally, you should be capable of contextualizing historical events and processes within wider regional, global, or chronological frameworks, showcasing your comprehension of the interrelated nature of world history.

- **Synthesis**

You should connect your arguments and examples to broader historical themes, time periods, or geographical contexts. This skill involves thinking critically and making connections between different aspects of world history, showcasing your ability to draw conclusions and identify overarching trends or patterns.

The scoring guidelines for the short-answer questions are designed to evaluate your proficiency in applying historical thinking skills, providing relevant and specific evidence, and demonstrating comprehension of the broader historical context.

For each short-answer question, a scoring scale of 0 to 3 points is utilized, with the following criteria:

- 1 point for identifying and addressing the question's specific task(s).
- 1 point for providing relevant and specific historical evidence to support your response.
- 1 point for demonstrating an understanding of the question's broader historical context or implications.

The scores for each short-answer question are combined to determine your total score for Part B.

The overall score for Section I is calculated by aggregating your scores from both Part A and Part B. The multiple-choice questions contribute 40% to the Section I score, while the short-answer questions contribute 20%. The total score for Section I is then converted into a weighted score, which accounts for 60% of your total AP World History Exam score.

Section II: Free Response

Section II comprises two types of questions:

1. Document-Based Question (DBQ)

The Document-Based Question (DBQ) is a key component of the AP World History Exam's Section II, which focuses on Free Response questions. This question type requires you to analyze a set of primary and secondary sources and use them to construct a coherent and well-supported argument in response to a historical question or prompt.

The DBQ is designed to test your ability to:

• Analyze and Interpret Various Types of Historical Documents

The Document-Based Question (DBQ) section will provide you with a range of primary and secondary sources, including written documents, images, maps, or graphs. Your objective is to conduct a thorough analysis of each source, extracting pertinent information and grasping the primary ideas, arguments, purpose, or viewpoint presented by the author. It is crucial to be mindful of any potential biases or constraints inherent in the source material. This entails critically evaluating the sources and being able to discern the author's intentions and the historical backdrop in which the sources were produced.

• Develop a Clear and Defensible Thesis Statement That Addresses the Prompt

To answer the DBQ effectively, you must craft a clear and concise thesis statement that directly addresses the historical question or prompt. This statement should outline your main argument and serve as the foundation for your essay.

• Use Evidence From The Provided Sources to Support Your Argument

Your essay should incorporate evidence from the documents to support your thesis statement and main points. You must analyze and interpret the sources, explain their relevance, and demonstrate how they support your argument. Be sure to provide appropriate citations or references to the documents in your essay.

• Consider The Historical Context and Differing Perspectives when Analyzing The Sources

While analyzing the documents, it is important to consider the wider historical context and the diverse perspectives or interpretations that may be present. Take into account any possible biases or limitations within the sources and contemplate how different perspectives can influence your comprehension of the topic.

The DBQ (Document-Based Question) is evaluated using a scoring scale ranging from 0 to 7 points, based on the following criteria:

- **Thesis/Claim (1 point):** Develop a clear, concise, and historically defensible thesis statement that directly addresses the prompt.
- **Contextualization (1 point):** Situate your argument within the broader historical context, demonstrating an understanding of the relevant historical events, developments, or processes.
- **Evidence from the documents (2 points):** Use evidence from at least six of the provided documents to support your argument. Analyze and interpret the sources, and explain their relevance to your thesis.
- **Evidence beyond the documents (1 point):** Provide additional historical evidence beyond the documents to support your argument, demonstrating your knowledge of the course content.
- **Analysis and reasoning (2 points):** Demonstrate your ability to apply historical thinking skills to analyze and interpret the evidence, evaluate multiple perspectives, or draw connections between different historical events or developments.

2. Long Essay Question (LEQ)

The Long Essay Question (LEQ) is another key component of the AP World History Exam's Section II, which focuses on Free Response questions. The LEQ asks you to develop a clear and nuanced argument in response to a historical question or prompt. You can choose one of three questions, each of which focuses on a different historical thinking skill, such as comparison, causation, or continuity and change over time.

The LEQ is designed to test your ability to:

• Develop a Clear and Defensible Thesis Statement That Addresses The Prompt

Crafting a clear and concise thesis statement is crucial to answering the LEQ effectively. Your thesis statement should directly address the historical question or prompt and serve as the foundation for your essay.

• Use Specific And Relevant Evidence From The Course Content to Support Your Argument

Your essay should be grounded in concrete historical evidence from the course material. This involves selecting appropriate examples, details, or data to support your argument and demonstrating a thorough understanding of the relevant historical context.

• Apply Historical Thinking Skills to Analyze Your Argument's Broader Context and Significance

The LEQ requires you to use one or more historical thinking skills to analyze and interpret historical events, developments, or processes. This may involve examining cause and effect relationships, comparing and contrasting different historical phenomena, or assessing changes and continuities over time.

The LEQ is scored on a scale of 0 to 6 points based on the following criteria:

   • **Thesis/Claim (1 point):** Develop a clear, concise, and historically defensible thesis statement that directly addresses the prompt.
   • **Contextualization (1 point):** Situate your argument within the broader historical context, demonstrating an understanding of the relevant historical events, developments, or processes.
   • **Evidence (2 points):** Use specific and relevant historical evidence from the course content to support your argument, demonstrating your knowledge of the relevant historical context.
   • **Analysis and reasoning (2 points):** Demonstrate your ability to apply historical thinking skills to analyze and interpret the evidence, evaluate multiple perspectives, or draw connections between different historical events or developments.

The main difference between the DBQ and LEQ lies in the source of evidence used to support the argument. The DBQ focuses on analyzing provided documents and integrating them into the argument, while the LEQ relies on students' own knowledge of world history to provide evidence and examples.

The overall score for Section II is calculated by combining your scores from the DBQ and the LEQ. The DBQ accounts for 25% of your total exam score, while the LEQ accounts for 15%. The total score for Section II is then converted into a weighted score, which accounts for 40% of your total AP World History Exam score.

The AP World History Exam does not have specific passing scores for each section. Instead, your scores from Section I (Multiple Choice and Short Answer) and Section II (Free Response) are combined and converted into a composite score. The composite score is then translated into a final AP score on a scale of 1 to 5.

The final AP scores are interpreted as follows:

1. No recommendation
2. Possibly qualified
3. Qualified
4. Well qualified
5. Extremely well qualified

A score of 3 or higher is typically regarded as passing, and depending on the specific policies of the college or university you attend, you might be eligible for advanced placement or college credit. However, some institutions may require a score of 4 or 5 to grant credit or advanced placement.

By understanding the format and structure of the AP World History Exam and how APWH is scored, you can increase your preparation for the test and score an approaching better score.

STRATEGIES FOR ANSWERING THE MULTIPLE-CHOICE QUESTIONS

The multiple-choice section of the AP World History exam can be a challenging component for many students. Nevertheless, there are effective strategies and approaches that can enhance your chances of selecting the correct answers and achieving a high score.

Consider the following key tactics:

1. Employing the Process of Elimination

Utilizing the process of elimination is a valuable tactic that can enhance your ability to answer multiple-choice questions accurately and efficiently. By systematically eliminating incorrect or improbable answer choices, you can narrow down your options and increase the likelihood of selecting the correct answer.

Here's how you can utilize this strategy effectively:

Step 1: Read the Question and Identify the Main Idea or Topic

Before delving into the process of elimination, it is crucial to grasp the main idea or topic the question is addressing. Understanding the context and any underlying biases or assumptions within the question can provide valuable insights. For instance, if the question inquires about the significant contributors to the rise of the Mongol Empire, it may offer historical context that sheds light on the events and circumstances leading to its ascent.

Step 2: Read Each Base or Keyword in the Question One by One

After identifying the main idea or topic and taking note of any biases or assumptions, you can proceed to examine each base word or keyword individually. This approach ensures that you capture all the relevant bases to which each aspect of the question relates. For instance, if the question pertains to various methods of acquiring slaves in Africa, you would carefully assess each base word separately to ensure a comprehensive understanding of the question. This allows you to consider all the potential avenues related to the acquisition of slaves in Africa. The bases could include: "A." Slavery? Yes," "B." Europeans? Yes, "C. A number of African kingdoms? Yes" If the question reads, "Which of the following was a key factor in the rise of the Mongol Empire?" you might read this question to identify all of the bases by reading each word separately.

Step 3. Select Alternates Based on Previous Reading and Information

After identifying all the bases, you can leverage the knowledge acquired from previous sections to aid in your decision-making process. For instance, if "A." Slavery? is one base for this question, but you are certain that this base does not apply because it deals with historical events that occurred centuries ago, then you should eliminate this choice as an answer. However, if you are uncertain about the relevance of "A." Slavery? You can also read this base to see if there is anything else in this question that may help you to identify possible answers that address slave trading in Africa. For example, "D. A number of African kingdoms? Yes." provides a possibility that you might have missed while reading the base words one by one.

Step 4: Read the Other Alternates and Determine the Most Likely Answer

Using what you have learned from previous sections and your selection of bases, now it is time to look at other alternatives to help determine which answer most likely best answers the question being asked. As an example, if one of the bases is "A. Slavery?", you may eliminate choices that do not mention slavery while considering the possibility that the question could be asking about the impact of slave trading on individuals who were already enslaved. This step is crucial as it allows you to more effectively identify the answer choice that is most likely correct, increasing your chances of answering a multiple-choice question accurately and swiftly. By eliminating options that do not align with the base or considering alternate interpretations, you can streamline the process and arrive at the most plausible answer more efficiently.

Step 5: Write Down Your Answer, Eliminate Consistent Alternatives, Choose the Correct Choice, and Proceed

Before proceeding to answer questions based on your knowledge from previous sections, there are a couple of final steps to optimize the use of this strategy for multiple-choice questions.

First, take a few minutes to jot down your answer choices and make note of the options you have eliminated. This step is crucial as it helps you recognize which answers align with your knowledge and eliminates incorrect choices, keeping consistent answers in mind.

Second, proceed systematically and carefully by thoroughly reading each question. Identify the potential correct answer(s), eliminate choices that contradict what you have already read, and then move on to the next question. This approach minimizes guesswork and maximizes your chances of answering correctly within the allotted time.

The process of elimination is a powerful strategy that enhances your ability to answer multiple-choice questions effectively and efficiently. It serves as a valuable tool to optimize your time during exams. Although it is not mandatory to always use this strategy, it enables you to swiftly narrow down options and reinforce your existing knowledge, enabling you to respond accordingly.

2. Identify Context Cues

Identifying context clues is another important strategy for answering multiple-choice AP World History Exam questions. Context clues can help you identify important information and narrow down the answer choices to those most likely correct.

Here are some tips for identifying and using context clues effectively:

• Pay Attention to The Verb Tense Used in The Question

Paying attention to the verb tense used in the question is important to identifying context clues in multiple-choice questions on the AP World History Exam. Verb tense can indeed provide valuable context clues that aid in selecting the correct answer.

For instance, in a question that examines the impact of a historical event or process, the use of past verb tense indicates a focus on the immediate or long-term effects. Conversely, the presence of present or present perfect verb tense suggests a question about the ongoing impact.

In a similar vein, when a question explores a historical trend or development, the use of past verb tense suggests a focus on the period leading up to the event or development. On the contrary, if the verb tense is in the present or present perfect, it suggests that the question relates to the ongoing nature of the trend or development.

By attentively observing the verb tense used in the question, one can identify significant contextual cues that assist in selecting the appropriate answer. This enables the exclusion of answer choices that do not align with the given time period or the scope of the question, allowing for a concentration on answer choices that are more likely to be accurate.

• Consider The Author's Perspective or Bias

In numerous instances, the person posing a question or the source material may have a specific viewpoint or inclination regarding the historical event, process, or theme being discussed.

When addressing multiple-choice questions, it is essential to consider the author's viewpoint or bias. This involves carefully reading the question and answer choices while taking into account any potential motivations or biases at play. This may entail observing language or tone that indicates a particular perspective or bias, or considering the historical context in which the question or source material was created.

For instance, if a question inquires about the causes of a historical event and one of the answer choices reflects a specific political or ideological standpoint, it may suggest bias. Similarly, if a question addresses the effects of a particular historical process and one of the answer choices employs overly positive or negative language, it could indicate bias.

Furthermore, if the question focuses on a specific historical theme and the answer choices showcase various possible perspectives relating to that theme, it may imply bias. For example, when dealing with a query related to the societal roles of women and one of the response options notably aligns with a feminist standpoint, it could imply a possibility of bias. In such cases, one must remember that authors advocating for a feminist stance might not fully capture all the nuances of feminist theories. Therefore, it is pivotal to opt for the response that best resonates with your personal viewpoints or ideologies.

By remaining cognizant of authorial perspectives or biases, one can approach multiple-choice questions critically, leading to more informed decisions rooted in a comprehensive understanding of the subject matter.

By considering the author's perspective or bias, one can identify significant contextual clues that aid in selecting the correct answer. This can help you more effectively eliminate answer choices that do not reflect your own perspective or bias and focus on answer choices that are most likely correct according to your own beliefs or perspectives.

- **Looking for Cause-and-Effect Relationships**

Cause-and-effect relationships refer to the correlations between events, processes, or phenomena, where one event triggers or impacts another. Grasping and remembering intricate and interconnected cause-and-effect relationships within historical events or processes can pose a significant challenge. Nevertheless, the ability to perceive and understand such correlations can certainly aid in determining the accurate answer in a multiple-choice question.

Detecting cause-and-effect links in a multiple-choice question requires meticulous reading of the query and attentive recognition of crucial words or phrases suggesting an association between happenings or procedures. Be vigilant for phrases such as *"led to," "caused,"* or *"had an impact on,"* that imply a cause-and-effect association.

To exemplify, think about a query focusing on the repercussions of the Industrial Revolution on labor structures. If one of the response options discusses the advent of novel factory equipment, it signifies a cause-and-effect correlation. The Industrial Revolution began with the introduction of new machines, which greatly impacted how individuals collaborated. The implementation of these machines necessitated that workers adapt to new technologies and working conditions, resulting in significant changes to their work processes. The implementation of new machinery was a critical factor in propelling the Industrial Revolution and exerted a substantial impact on labor relations. Workers had to adapt to the new technology and working conditions, leading to notable shifts in their employment dynamics.

Similarly, if a question examines the commercialization of society and one answer choice refers to the adoption of new advertising methods to increase sales, it suggests a cause-and-effect relationship. The introduction of new advertising methods boosted sales, subsequently leading to further commercialization and distinguishing modern society from traditional ones.

By identifying cause-and-effect relationships in questions and analyzing the context in which a particular answer choice appears, you can focus on options that likely reflect such relationships. This helps in effectively eliminating choices that lack cause-and-effect connections and concentrates on the most plausible correct answer.

Comprehending the chronological order is indeed crucial for understanding the causes, effects, and overall significance of historical events. Considering the chronology is indeed a valuable tool in selecting the correct answer in a multiple-choice question.

To infuse the concept of time order into a multiple-choice query, it's crucial to examine the question carefully and pinpoint words or phrases that denote a particular historical period or sequence of events. Search for terms which frame a chronological context, like *"during the Middle Ages," "in the 19th century,"* or *"post-Roman Empire."*

For instance, if a query centers around the evolution of trade pathways in the ancient era and one of the response options refers to the Silk Road, it implies that the answer might be related to the span from around 200 BCE to 200 CE when the Silk Road was instrumental in connecting China with the Mediterranean region.

Similarly, if a question investigates the catalysts of the French Revolution and one of the alternatives indicates Louis XVI's reign, it suggests that the answer likely refers to the period when Louis XVI held the throne in France, approximately from 1774 to 1792. In this phase, multiple influences instigated the French Revolution.

By thoughtfully evaluating the order of presentation of the questions and scrutinizing the contextual clues provided for each response option, one can filter the choices and focus on those that correspond with the chronological progression of events or procedures.

By meticulously considering the order in which the questions are presented and carefully analyzing the contextual information provided for each answer choice, one can narrow down the options and focus on those that align with the chronological progression of events or processes.

- **Use Process of Elimination in Combination with Context Clues**

This strategy entails utilizing context clues to narrow down the possibilities and subsequently employing the process of elimination to select the correct answer.

To effectively implement this strategy, it is crucial to engage in attentive reading of both the question and the answer choices. Identify any contextual hints that can aid in selecting the correct answer. By incorporating elements such as being attentive to verb tense, considering the author's perspective or bias, identifying cause-and-effect relationships, and being mindful of chronology, among other factors, you can enhance your ability to make accurate choices in multiple-choice questions. This process involves taking these factors into account during your analysis, enabling you to make more informed and precise selections.

After identifying any pertinent context clues, you can use the process of elimination to eliminate answer options that do not fit the question's context. For instance, you can disregard answer choices that do not correspond to the specified time period or sequence of events, or that do not adequately address the topic or theme being examined.

After eliminating answer choices that are incompatible with the question's context, you can rely on your knowledge and comprehension of the subject to choose the correct answer from the remaining options. This may involve analyzing the remaining answer choices to determine which one is the most accurate, relevant, or comprehensive. Applying logical reasoning and maintaining a logical thought process can indeed assist in identifying the answer choice that is most likely to be correct.

It is essential to acknowledge and be aware of personal biases when approaching multiple-choice questions. Recognizing these biases can help approach the questions with a more objective mindset, enabling evaluation of answer choices based on their merit rather than personal preferences.

As previously mentioned, guessing the correct answer without any context clues or prior knowledge is unlikely to yield successful results. Rather than relying solely on personal biases, it is advisable to rely on your understanding of the subject matter to narrow down options and identify the correct answer from the remaining choices. Thorough comprehension of each question and thoughtful consideration of all options will increase the likelihood of selecting the correct answer.

Context clues indeed play a crucial role in reinforcing existing knowledge of historical events or processes and deepening understanding of their causes, effects, and significance. While identifying context clues is only one of the many strategies that can be employed to excel in the AP World History Exam, it is a valuable tool that can enhance performance and contribute to achieving the highest possible score. You can develop a strong ability to recognize context clues and use them effectively to answer multiple-choice exam questions with practice and attention to detail.

3. Identify Patterns and Themes

Another valuable strategy for answering multiple-choice questions on the AP World History exam is identifying historical patterns and themes. By grasping recurring themes and patterns, you can utilize this knowledge to respond to questions that pertain to diverse time periods or regions. This approach requires a solid grasp of historical concepts and their interconnectedness.

Here's how you can execute this strategy:

Step 1: Gain Proficiency in Key Historical Themes and Progressions

Alongside comprehending specific historical occurrences, dedicate time to studying overarching themes and progressions. Examples include revolutions, migrations, technological advancements, and cultural exchanges. This comprehensive understanding will provide you with a broader outlook on history, enabling you to identify recurring patterns and themes more readily.

Step 2: Analyze the Question for Patterns or Themes

When presented with a multiple-choice question, carefully read the question and look for clues that may hint at underlying patterns or themes. This will often involve analyzing the time period, region, and events mentioned in the question.

Let's consider a question that might be presented as follows:

"Which of the following factors played a role in the decline of both the Roman Empire and the Han Dynasty?" It is crucial to discern that this question seeks patterns concerning the downfall of these significant empires.

Step 3: Apply Your Knowledge of Patterns and Themes

After identifying the relevant patterns or themes in the question, apply your knowledge of these concepts to help you evaluate the answer choices.

Regarding the previous question about the downfall of the Roman Empire and the Han Dynasty, some factors to contemplate include:

- Internal political instability
- Economic issues such as inflation or excessive taxation
- Social unrest and rebellions
- External pressures, such as invasions or migrations

With these factors in mind, you can now evaluate the answer choices to determine which one best describes a common factor contributing to the fall of both empires.

Step 4: Practice Identifying Patterns and Themes

The more you practice identifying patterns and themes, the better you will become at recognizing them during the exam. As you study, try connecting different historical events and developments to broader historical patterns and themes.

Example:

While studying the Age of Exploration, you might notice a pattern of European nations seeking to expand their influence and control over new territories for economic and political reasons. This pattern can then be connected to other instances of expansion and imperialism throughout history, such as the Roman Empire's conquests or the colonization of Africa by European powers.

By mastering the skill of identifying patterns and themes, you will be better equipped to tackle multiple-choice questions on the AP World History exam. This skill allows you to recognize connections between historical events, time periods, and regions, helping you to effectively evaluate answer choices and select the most accurate response.

4. Time Management and Pacing

Effective time management and pacing are essential strategies for answering multiple-choice AP World History exam questions. With limited time to complete the exam, it's crucial to use your time efficiently and maintain a steady pace throughout the test.

Here's how to develop time management and pacing skills for answering multiple-choice section of the AP World History:

Step 1: Familiarize Yourself with the Exam Format and Timing

Before the exam, understand the format and timing of the multiple-choice section. The multiple-choice section for the AP World History exam consists of 55 questions to be completed in 55 minutes. This gives you approximately one minute per question.

Step 2: Develop a Personal Pacing Strategy

Developing a personal pacing strategy involves finding a balance between speed and accuracy that works best for you during the multiple-choice section of the AP World History exam.

To customize your pacing approach, consider the following recommendations and guidelines:

- **Assess Your Areas of Proficiency and Improvement**

Start by evaluating your strengths and weaknesses within the curriculum. Identify the areas where you feel most confident and those that require additional attention. Comprehending your areas of proficiency and limitations can aid in utilizing your exam time more efficiently. For example, you find questions related to economic systems more challenging. In that case, you should allot more time for these questions while moving more quickly through questions on topics you are more comfortable with.

- **Divide and Allocate Time**

You have approximately one minute per question-based on the 55-minute time limit for the multiple-choice section and the 55 questions. However, you should divide your time differently depending on your personal preferences and strengths. For instance, you could spend 45 seconds on easier questions and 75 seconds on more difficult ones, leaving 5 minutes in the end for review.

- **Practice Using Your Strategy**

Once you've developed your personal pacing strategy, practice using it with timed practice exams. By implementing strategic pacing and adapting your approach, you can boost your confidence and efficiency. Take note of any challenges you encounter, such as consistently running out of time or feeling rushed, and make appropriate adjustments to your strategy.

- **Prioritize Questions**

As you work through the multiple-choice section, prioritize answering questions that are easier or more familiar to you first. This ensures you maximize your score by answering questions you will get right. Save more difficult questions for later when you can dedicate more time to them without sacrificing points on easier questions.

- **Stay Flexible and Adaptive**

During the actual exam, be prepared to adapt your pacing strategy as needed. Some questions may demand more time to answer, while others can be resolved quickly. Being aware of the allocated time and adapting your pace accordingly is important to ensure that you can answer all the questions within the given time limit.

To enhance efficiency, it is advisable to create a personalized pacing strategy that considers your individual strengths, weaknesses, and preferences. This strategy will assist you in effectively managing your time and optimizing your performance, enabling you to utilize the allocated exam time to its fullest extent.

Step 3: Practice Pacing with Practice Exams

Take practice exams to improve your pacing skills. Try to simulate the actual testing conditions when taking practice exams. This means finding a quiet space, using a timer, and sticking to the same time constraints as the actual exam. After completing a practice exam, it is beneficial to conduct a thorough review of your answers and evaluate your performance. Dedicate time to analyze the questions you answered correctly, those you answered incorrectly, and the ones you left unanswered. Seek patterns in your errors and reflect on whether they are linked to particular content areas, question types, or pacing concerns. This analysis will help you adjust your pacing strategy and focus your study efforts on areas that need improvement.

Based on your performance analysis, make adjustments to your pacing strategy if necessary. For example, consider speeding up your pace or prioritizing easier questions if you need more time. If you're finishing with plenty of time to spare but making careless mistakes, slow down and focus more on accuracy. The objective is to achieve a suitable equilibrium between swiftness and precision that suits your individual preferences.

In each practice exam, apply your pacing strategy, review your performance, and make necessary adjustments. This repetition will enhance your comfort with pacing and improve your ability to answer questions efficiently and accurately within time constraints.

Step 4: Skip Difficult Questions and Return Later

Postponing challenging questions and revisiting them later can be an effective tactic for managing your time efficiently. To maximize efficiency within the given time limit, the aim is to allocate a specific time frame to each question, prioritizing the completion of as many questions as possible.

Here are some effective strategies to implement this approach:

• Read Each Question Carefully

As you work through the multiple-choice section, read each question carefully to determine its difficulty level. If you immediately recognize that a question is challenging or time-consuming, make a mental or physical note to return to it later.

• Mark Difficult Questions

Create a system for flagging challenging questions that you plan to revisit later. You can use a pencil to make a small mark on the question, circle the question number, or employ any other method that suits your preferences. It is essential to establish a consistent and easily recognizable marking system to swiftly identify the questions when you come back to them. This approach will help you manage your time effectively and prioritize your efforts during the exam.

• Move on Quickly

After marking a difficult question, move on to the next question without hesitation. Bear in mind that the primary aim is to answer as many questions as feasible within the given timeframe, making it crucial to refrain from dedicating too much time to a single question.

- **Allocate Time for Review**

As you develop your pacing strategy, make sure to allocate some time at the end of the multiple-choice section for reviewing and answering the difficult questions you skipped. Depending on your overall pacing, this could be from 5 to 10 minutes or more.

- **Return to Skipped Questions**

Once you have answered all of the easier questions, use your remaining time to return to the difficult questions you marked earlier. With the pressure of answering the other questions lifted, you can now approach the difficult questions with a clearer mind and a better understanding of the material.

- **Use Remaining Time Wisely**

If you find yourself with extra time after addressing the more challenging questions, it is advisable to utilize that time for reviewing your answers and verifying their accuracy. Utilize this opportunity to review your work, double-checking that all questions have been answered accurately. Take note of any necessary corrections or adjustments before the time limit elapses. This comprehensive review can help minimize errors and boost your confidence in the accuracy of your responses.

By implementing the strategy of skipping difficult questions and returning to them later, you can effectively manage your time during the multiple-choice section of the AP World History exam. This approach can prevent being bogged down by challenging questions and guarantee that you have the chance to respond to as many questions as possible within the allotted time. It is crucial to highlight demanding questions, reserve some time for review, and utilize the remaining time efficiently to maximize your likelihood of success on the exam.

Effective time management and pacing are critical strategies for answering multiple-choice questions on exams like the AP World History exam. By integrating these strategies into your exam preparation and applying them during the actual test, you can maximize your score by answering as many questions as possible within the allocated time while maintaining accuracy.

Efficient implementation of these tactics can result in notable enhancements in your performance on multiple-choice tests, thereby increasing your likelihood of success. Ensure to practice and become familiar with these strategies to optimize your exam experience.

Sample Multiple-Choice Questions With Answer

1. During the era spanning 600 to 1450 CE, what technical development contributed most substantially to the proliferation of commerce and the birth of fresh financial structures?

A)Astrolabe
B)Magnetic compass
C)Press for printing
D)Wheel for spinning

Answer: Option B

2. What was a significant commonality shared by the Aztec and Inca Empires in the 15th century?

A)Both civilizations involved human sacrifice within their religious observances.
B)Both kingdoms depended largely on sea trade for their economic wealth.
C)Both realms maintained a centralized bureaucratic governance system.
D)Both territories were chiefly Islamic in their religious practices.

Answer: Option A

3. What was a notable outcome of the Columbian Exchange during the 16th and 17th centuries?

A) Introduction of new staple crops such as wheat and rice to the Americas.

B) Creation of a global trading network revolving around the Indian Ocean.

C) Decline of feudalism and ascendancy of absolute monarchies in Europe.

D) Formation of large-scale multinational corporations controlling global trade.

Answer: Option A

4. Which option accurately encapsulates the influence of the Kyoto Protocol on international environmental policy throughout the 1990s and 2000s?

A) The formulation of global standards and goals for curtailing greenhouse gas emissions

B) The triggering of global political and economic instability, leading to prevalent societal disquiet

C) The expansion of global capitalism and the growth of multinational corporations

D) The rise of innovative political and religious movements contesting traditional power hierarchies

Answer: Option A

5. Which of the following was a significant impact of the rise of social media on global society during the 2000s and 2010s?

A) The endorsement of international collaboration and the institution of global governance entities

B) The emergence of new platforms for communication, information sharing, and social interaction

C) The destabilization of political and economic systems worldwide, leading to widespread social unrest

D) The establishment of new political and economic systems promoting social equality and democracy

Answer: Option B

6. What had a substantial effect on the Enlightenment in the 18th century?

A) Ottoman Empire's expansion into Europe.

B) Rise in usage of enslaved labor within the Americas.

C) Promotion of democratic ideals and political reforms.

D) Decline of international trade and ascension of economic isolationism.

Answer: Option C

7. How would you describe the Ottoman Empire's political system at its zenith during the 16th century?

A) A decentralized confederation of semi-independent city-states.

B) A theocratic monarchy led by a religious leader, known as a caliph.

C) A constitutional republic with a representative parliament.

D) An absolute monarchy with centralized administration and a professional bureaucracy.

Answer: Option D

8. What was a considerable cause of the Mughal Empire's decline in the 18th century?

A)Ascendancy of European colonial powers and their increasing influence in India.

B)A series of catastrophic natural disasters, such as droughts and famines.

C)Forced conversion of the predominantly Hindu populace to Islam.

D)Emergence of powerful indigenous resistance movements within the Americas.

Answer: Option A

9. Which of the provided options best describes the relationship between China's Ming Dynasty and the Japanese shogunate during the 14th and 15th centuries?

A)A tight alliance based on shared political and economic interests.

B)A strained rivalry characterized by frequent military conflicts and territorial disputes.

C)A limited exchange of goods and ideas facilitated by the tribute system.

D)A total absence of contact and isolation from one another.

Answer: Option C

10. What economic system was strongly tied to the growth of European empires during the 16th and 17th centuries?

A)Capitalism
B)Feudalism
C)Socialism
D)Mercantilism

Answer: Option D

11. Which of the provided answer options gives the most accurate portrayal of how the Atlantic slave trade affected African societies from the 16th to the 19th centuries?

A)Widespread adoption of European languages and customs.

B)Rise of powerful centralized states controlling the slave trade.

C)Depopulation and destabilization of numerous African communities.

D)Establishment of democratic institutions and political reforms.

Answer: Option C

12. What was a major factor influencing the French Revolution (1789-1799)?

A)The decline of the Spanish and Portuguese empires in the Americas.

B)Dissemination of nationalism and revolutionary ideals throughout Europe.

C)Establishment of a global trading network revolving around the Indian Ocean.

D)Rise of large multinational corporations dominating global trade.

Answer: Option B

13. What was a key characteristic of the social structure in most European societies during the 18th century?

A)Emergence of a large and educated middle class.

B)Dominance of a hereditary aristocracy.

C)Ascension of a powerful military caste.

D)Decline of urban populations in favor of rural communities.

Answer: Option B

14. What was a significant factor that enabled European influence to expand in Asia during the 16th and 17th centuries?

A) Development of new maritime technologies that facilitated long-distance travel.

B) Decline of the Mongol Empire and the resulting power vacuum in Asia.

C) Spread of Christianity and establishment of European religious institutions.

D) Formation of alliances between European powers and indigenous Asian states.

Answer: Option A

15. What was the primary objective of the Berlin Conference (1884-1885) within the context of European imperialism?

A)To create a system for the peaceful colonization of Africa by European powers.

B)To mediate disputes between European powers over their respective colonial possessions in Asia.

C)To form a coalition of European powers to resist the expansion of the Ottoman Empire.

D)To establish an international trade organization to regulate global commerce and protect European economic interests.

Answer: Option A

16. What was a significant impact of World War I on global society?

A) Promotion of a novel, inclusive global order with enhanced democratic principles.

B) Formation of the United Nations as an international governing body.

C) Rise of the United States as a prominent global force.

D) Destabilization of political and economic systems in Europe and beyond.

Answer: Option D

17. How did the Great Depression affect global society in the 1930s?

A) Increase in authoritarian regimes and decline of democracy.

B) Spread of socialist and communist ideologies globally.

C) Emergence of global consumer culture and growth of multinational corporations.

D) Promotion of international cooperation and expansion of global trade.

Answer: Option A

18. What was a significant impact of World War II on global society?

A) Formation of the European Union as a regional alliance for economic and political purposes.

B) Rise of the United States as a dominant global power.

C) Decline of colonial empires and rise of national liberation movements.

D) Development of new technologies revolutionizing medicine and transportation.

Answer: Option C

19. What was a significant impact of the Cold War on global society?

A) Spread of democratic ideals and promotion of human rights worldwide.

B) Creation of the European Union as a prominent political and economic force.

C) Rise of the United States as a dominant global power.

D) Proliferation of nuclear weapons and threat of global annihilation.

Answer: Option D

20. Which statement best characterizes the effect of the Great Recession on the world economy during the late 2000s and early 2010s?

A) The encouragement of international commerce and global economic collaboration

B) The unsettling of global financial markets and economies, leading to extensive joblessness and economic difficulties

C) The inception of new political and economic structures advocating social equality and democracy

D) The expansion of global capitalism and the growth of multinational corporations

Answer: Option B

21. What among the answer options below had a significant role in the collapse of the Soviet Union in 1991?

A) Decline of communism as a global ideological force.

B) Increasing influence of the United States in Eastern Europe.

C) Emergence of novel technologies revolutionizing the global economy.

D) Failure of Soviet leaders to address economic and political issues within the country.

Answer: Option D

22. Which factor had a substantial influence on the civil rights movement in the United States during the 1950s and 1960s?

A) The enactment of fresh laws and policies fostering racial equality and social justice

B) The advocacy for economic nationalism and the expansion of protectionist measures

C) The destabilization of political and economic infrastructures in the United States, inciting widespread societal turmoil

D) The rise of novel political and religious movements contesting established power structures

Answer: Option A

23. What answer choice best portrays the influence of the Arab Spring on the Middle East and North Africa?

A) Establishment of democratic institutions and promotion of human rights.

B) Emergence of new religious and cultural movements challenging traditional power structures.

C) Destabilization of political and economic systems in the region, leading to widespread conflict and violence.

D) Promotion of economic development and expansion of trade and commerce.

Answer: Option C

24. What answer choice best describes the impact of the global COVID-19 pandemic on the world in 2020 and 2021?

A) Acceleration of globalization and growth of multinational corporations.

B) Promotion of international cooperation and establishment of a global health governing body.

C) Destabilization of political and economic systems globally, leading to widespread unemployment and social unrest.

D) Emergence of new technologies revolutionizing how people work and communicate.

Answer: Option C

25. What factors molded the American Civil Rights Movement during the 1950s and 1960s?

A) The implementation of laws promoting civil rights and racial parity.

B) Promotion of socialist and communist ideologies in the United States.

C) Expansion of the American economy and growth of multinational corporations.

D) Emergence of new technologies transforming American society and culture.

Answer: Option A

26. Which best articulates the influence of the feminist movement on Western societies in the 20th century?

A) The creation of legislation and policies advancing gender parity and women's rights.

B) The decline of traditional family structures and the rise of alternative lifestyles

C) The emergence of new technologies that transformed the way women work and live

D) The promotion of new religious and cultural movements that challenged traditional gender roles

Answer: Option A

27. Which aspect notably shaped the Green Revolution in the mid-20th century?

A)The endorsement of sustainable agricultural methods and natural resource conservation.

B)The amplification of global food production and the curtailment of global hunger.

C)The waning of traditional farming systems and the proliferation of multinational agribusinesses.

D)The advent of new technologies that revolutionized the production and consumption of food.

Answer: Option B

28. Which of the following answer choices best characterizes the effect of the Internet on global society during the late 20th and early 21st centuries?

A)The homogenization of cultures and the decline of local traditions

B)The expansion of economic opportunities and the growth of multinational corporations

C)The emergence of new technologies that have transformed communication and information sharing

D)The increasing isolationism and protectionism of many countries around the world

Answer: Option C

29. Which element notably shaped the Industrial Revolution in Western societies during the 18th and 19th centuries?

A) The creation of novel political and economic structures advocating social parity and democracy

B) The promotion of traditional agricultural practices and the conservation of natural resources

C) The decline of urban populations and the growth of rural communities

D) The emergence of new technologies that transformed the way goods were produced and consumed

Answer: Option D

30. Which best characterizes the influence of the European Renaissance on Western societies from the 14th to the 17th centuries?

A) The establishment of new religious and cultural movements promoting artistic expression and humanism

B) The promotion of traditional feudal systems and the decline of individualism

C) The advent of innovative technologies that revolutionized people's work and life routines

D) The creation of new political and economic structures advocating social parity and democracy

Answer: Option A

31. Which was a significant consequence of the French Revolution on worldwide society in the late 18th and early 19th centuries?

A) The promotion of democratic ideals and political reforms worldwide

B) The decline of traditional political structures and the rise of authoritarian regimes

C) The expansion of global trade and the growth of multinational corporations

D)The advent of innovative technologies that revolutionized people's work and life routines

Answer: Option A

32. Which best articulates the influence of the Protestant Reformation on Western societies during the 16th century?

A)The promotion of religious diversity and tolerance worldwide

B)The decline of traditional religious structures and the rise of secularism

C)The advent of innovative technologies that revolutionized people's work and life routines

D)The creation of new political and economic structures advocating social parity and democracy

Answer: Option B

33. Which of the following significantly impacted the Age of Exploration on global society during the 15th to 18th centuries?

A)The establishment of new political and economic systems promoting global trade and colonialism

B)The promotion of religious and cultural diversity worldwide

C)The decline of traditional agricultural practices and the growth of urbanization

D)The advent of innovative technologies that revolutionized people's work and life routines

Answer: Option A

34. Which best characterizes the influence of the Scientific Revolution on Western societies during the 16th to 18th centuries?

A)The promotion of religious and cultural diversity worldwide

B)The creation of new political and economic structures advocating social parity and democracy

C)The advent of innovative technologies that revolutionized people's work and life routines

D)The establishment of new scientific theories and discoveries that challenged traditional beliefs and knowledge

Answer: Option D

35. Which of the following was a significant impact of the American Revolution on global society during the late 18th century?

A)The promotion of democratic ideals and political reforms worldwide

B)The decline of traditional political structures and the rise of authoritarian regimes

C)The expansion of global trade and the growth of multinational corporations

D)The advent of innovative technologies that revolutionized people's work and life routines

Answer: Option A

36. Which describes how the Civil War affected 19th-century American society?

A) The creation of new political and economic structures advocating social parity and democracy

B) The decline of traditional political structures and the rise of authoritarian regimes

C) The promotion of religious and cultural diversity worldwide

D) The disruption of political and economic structures in the United States, triggering extensive social unrest

Answer: Option A

37. Which of the following significantly impacted World War II's global economy?

A) The advocacy for international commerce and global economic collaboration

B) The obliteration of global economic infrastructure and the advent of new political and economic structures

C) The creation of multinational corporations and the growth of global capitalism

D) The endorsement of economic nationalism and the expansion of protectionist policies

Answer: Option B

38. Which best describes how the Cold War shaped 20th-century international politics and diplomacy?

A)The endorsement of global collaboration and the creation of worldwide governing entities

B)The emergence of new political and economic systems promoting social equality and democracy

C)The destabilization of political and economic systems worldwide, leading to widespread conflict and violence

D)The formation of alliances between countries and the expansion of military and nuclear arsenals

Answer: Option D

39. How did the Vietnam War impact 1960s and 1970s American society?

A)The endorsement of global collaboration and the creation of worldwide governing entities

B)The creation of new political and economic systems endorsing social equality and democracy

C)The disruption of political and economic structures in the United States, triggering extensive social unrest

D)The proliferation of global commerce and the growth of multinational corporations

Answer: Option C

40. Which best characterizes the influence of the Reagan administration on American politics and diplomacy in the 1980s?

A)The endorsement of global collaboration and the creation of worldwide governing entities

B)The enhancement of American military and economic power and the pursuit of conservative policies

C)The disruption of political and economic structures in the United States, triggering extensive social unrest

D)The creation of new political and economic systems endorsing social equality and democracy

Answer: Option B

41. What was a notable consequence of the Gulf War on the global economy in the 1990s?

A)The promotion of international trade and economic cooperation worldwide

B)The creation of new political and economic systems endorsing social equality and democracy

C)The destabilization of political and economic systems worldwide, leading to widespread conflict and violence

D)The expansion of global capitalism and the growth of multinational corporations

Answer: Option A

42. Which best describes how 9/11 affected American society in the 2000s?

A)American military strength and conservative policies

B)The endorsement of global collaboration and the creation of worldwide governing entities

C)The disruption of political and economic structures in the United States, triggering extensive social unrest

D)The proliferation of global commerce and the growth of multinational corporations

Answer: Option A

43. Which of the following was a significant impact of the Arab Spring on global politics and diplomacy during the 2010s?

A)The creation of new political and economic structures advocating social parity and democracy

B)The political and economic upheavals in the Middle East and North Africa, resulting in considerable disorder and conflicts.

C)The promotion of international trade and economic cooperation worldwide

D)The emergence of new political and religious movements challenging traditional power structures

Answer: Option B

44. Which answer choice best illustrates the effect of the Black Lives Matter movement on American society during the 2010s and 2020s?

A)The creation of new laws and policies advocating racial parity and social justice

B)The endorsement of economic nationalism and the expansion of protectionist policies

C)The disruption of political and economic structures in the United States, triggering extensive social unrest

D)The emergence of new political and religious movements challenging traditional power structures

Answer: Option A

45. Which of the following answer choices represents a significant effect of the COVID-19 pandemic on the global economy during the 2020s?

A)The promotion of international trade and economic cooperation worldwide

B)The creation of new political and economic structures advocating social parity and democracy

C)The destabilization of global supply chains and the emergence of new economic models

D)The expansion of global capitalism and the growth of multinational corporations

Answer: Option C

46. Which best articulates the influence of the Me Too movement on American society during the 2010s and 2020s?

A)The creation of new laws and policies advocating gender parity and social justice

B)The endorsement of economic nationalism and the expansion of protectionist policies

C)The disruption of political and economic structures in the United States, triggering extensive social unrest

D)The emergence of new political and religious movements challenging traditional power structures

Answer: Option A

47. Which of the following was a significant impact of the Brexit referendum on British society and the global economy?

A)The promotion of international trade and economic cooperation worldwide

B)The political and economic turbulence in the United Kingdom and the European Union resulting in destabilization

C)The creation of new political and economic structures advocating social parity and democracy

D)The expansion of global capitalism and the growth of multinational corporations

Answer: Option B

48. Which of the following answer choices best characterizes the effect of the Black Lives Matter protests on American society during the summer of 2020?

A)The creation of new laws and policies advocating racial equality and social justice

B)The endorsement of economic nationalism and the expansion of protectionist policies

C)The disruption of political and economic structures in the United States, triggering extensive social unrest

D)The emergence of new political and religious movements challenging traditional power structures

Answer: Option A

49. What was a significant consequence of the #MeToo movement on American society during the 2010s and 2020s?

A)The creation of new laws and policies advocating gender parity and social justice

B)The endorsement of economic nationalism and the expansion of protectionist policies

C)The disruption of political and economic structures in the United States, triggering extensive social unrest

D)The emergence of new political and religious movements challenging traditional power structures

Answer: Option A

50. Which of the following answer options provides the most accurate portrayal of how the Black Lives Matter movement influenced global politics and diplomacy during the 2010s and 2020s?

A)The endorsement of global collaboration and the creation of worldwide governing entities

B)The disruption of political and economic structures in the United States, triggering extensive social unrest

C)The creation of new political and economic structures advocating social parity and democracy

D)The emergence of new political and religious movements challenging traditional power structures

Answer: Option B

51. How did the 2010s Occupy Wall Street movement affect American society?

A)New economic and social justice laws and policies

B)The endorsement of economic nationalism and the expansion of protectionist policies

C)The disruption of political and economic structures in the United States, triggering extensive social unrest

D)The emergence of new political and religious movements challenging traditional power structures

Answer: Option A

52. Which best articulates the influence of the Paris climate agreement on global environmental policy during the 2010s?

A)The endorsement of global collaboration and the creation of worldwide governing entities

B)The disruption of political and economic structures in the United States, triggering extensive social unrest

C)The creation of new political and economic systems advocating social equality and democracy

D)The expansion of global capitalism and the growth of multinational corporations

Answer: Option A

53. Which of the following significantly impacted the 2015 migrant crisis on European society and politics?

A)The establishment of new laws and policies promoting multiculturalism and diversity

B)The endorsement of economic nationalism and the expansion of protectionist policies

C)The destabilization of political and economic systems in Europe, leading to widespread social unrest

D)The emergence of new political and religious movements challenging traditional power structures

Answer: Option C

54. Which of the following answer choices best characterizes the effect of the legalization of same-sex marriage in the United States during the 2010s?

A)The establishment of new laws and policies promoting LGBTQ+ rights and social justice

B)The endorsement of economic nationalism and the expansion of protectionist policies

C)The disruption of political and economic structures in the United States, triggering extensive social unrest

D)The emergence of new political and religious movements challenging traditional power structures

Answer: Option A

55. Which option best characterizes the effect of the War on Terror on international politics and diplomacy during the 2000s and 2010s?

A) The endorsement of international cooperation and the creation of global governing agencies

B) The enlargement of American military prowess and the execution of contentious security actions

C) The upsetting of political and economic systems in the United States, leading to broad societal unrest

D) The growth of global commerce and the proliferation of multinational corporations.

Answer: Option B

MASTERING THE SAQ (SHORT ANSWER QUESTION)

The Short Answer Question (SAQ) section assesses a student's ability to analyze primary and secondary sources and articulate their knowledge of historical concepts concisely and effectively. While mastering the art of writing high-scoring SAQs is a very useful skill, the first step is to understand what is expected of you.

1. Dissecting the Question and Identifying Key Terms

The first thing to do is to break down the question into smaller components. It is a crucial step in understanding and answering SAQs effectively. This process allows you to break down the question, determine its requirements, and identify the specific concepts and themes it addresses.

Here's a step-by-step approach to dissecting a question and identifying key terms:

Step 1: Read The Question Carefully

Carefully read the entire question to grasp its meaning and requirements. It is important to comprehend the task the question requires of you. Take note of any specific guidelines provided, such as "compare," "contrast," "analyze," or "explain."

Step 2: Highlight or Underline Important Words or Phrases

As you read, underline or highlight the key terms and phrases that are central to the question. These could be historical periods, events, people, concepts, or analytical categories (such as cause and effect, continuity and change, or comparison).

Step 3: Define Key Terms

Define the key terms you've identified to ensure you clearly understand their meaning and relevance to the question. This may require referring to your course materials or conducting further research.

Step 4: Rephrase The Question in Your Own Words

To ensure you fully understand the question, rephrase it in your own words. This helps clarify the question's requirements and highlights any areas where you need additional information or understanding.

Step 5: Determine The Question's Analytical Focus

Identify the specific analytical task the question is asking you to perform. This may involve comparing and contrasting two historical phenomena, analyzing the causes or effects of an event, or examining the continuity and change over time. Understanding the analytical focus will help you structure your response and select appropriate evidence.

Step 6: Connect the Question to Broader Historical Themes and Context

Consider how the question relates to broader historical themes, trends, and concepts you've studied. Identifying these connections will help you provide appropriate contextual information in your response and demonstrate a deeper understanding of the topic.

This process will enable you to craft a focused, coherent, and well-supported answer that addresses the question's requirements and demonstrates your understanding of the historical context.

2. Crafting a Focused and Coherent Response

After carefully dissecting and defining the question, it's important to craft a focused and coherent response. It involves addressing each part of the question directly and providing evidence or examples to support your assertions.

Here's a step-by-step guide to crafting a focused and coherent response using an example question:

Example Question:

"Analyze the similarities and differences between the political structures of ancient Egypt and Mesopotamia."

Step 1: Address Each Part of the Question Directly and Explicitly

Make sure to address both the similarities and differences in your response. State your main points clearly and directly, ensuring they answer the question.

For example, start your response with an introductory statement that outlines your main points, such as, "Centralized political organizations were present in both ancient Egypt and Mesopotamia, yet they exhibited significant differences in their governance styles and rulership principles."

Step 2: Provide Specific Evidence or Examples to Support Your Assertions

Use concrete evidence and examples to back up your claims about the similarities and differences between the political structures of ancient Egypt and Mesopotamia.

For example, provide evidence for your claim about centralized political structures, such as, "Egypt was marked by a cohesive government led by a solitary ruler, the Pharaoh, contrasting with Mesopotamia's fragmented collection of city-states, each governed by individual leaders."

Step 3: Demonstrate an Understanding of The Historical Context and How it Relates to the Question

Show that you understand the broader historical context and can connect it to the specific question being asked.

For example, explain the concept of divine kingship in Egypt and how it influenced their political structure: "The political framework of Egypt was built on the principle of divine monarchy, assigning godlike status to the Pharaoh."

Step 4: Organize Your Response Logically and Coherently

Structure your response in a clear, logical manner that effectively communicates your main points. Use paragraphs to separate different ideas and ensure there is a clear progression of ideas from one point to the next.

Example:

- Begin with an introduction that outlines your main points.
- Provide a paragraph discussing the similarities between the political structures of ancient Egypt and Mesopotamia.
- Follow with a paragraph discussing the differences between the political structures of the two civilizations.
- To end your answer, it is essential to provide a summary of your key arguments and their relevance or significance.

Step 5: Be Concise And To The Point

Keep your response focused and concise, as each SAQ should be a maximum of a few paragraphs in length. Avoid unnecessary details or tangents and stick to the specific question being asked.

For example, in your conclusion, you might write, "To conclude, while centralized political systems were a feature of both ancient Egypt and Mesopotamia, the way power was structured and rulership was conceived differed significantly, echoing their unique cultural and religious environments."

Here's a suggested answer for the example question:

"Centralized political organizations were present in both ancient Egypt and Mesopotamia, yet they exhibited significant differences in their governance styles and rulership principles. Egypt was marked by a cohesive government led by a solitary ruler, the Pharaoh, contrasting with Mesopotamia's fragmented collection of city-states, each governed by individual leaders. The political architecture of Egypt was anchored on the idea of divine monarchy, endowing the Pharaoh with a deity's attributes. On the other hand, Mesopotamian leaders were perceived as mediators between their subjects and deities, tasked with preserving peace and conducting religious rites to pacify the gods. To conclude, while centralized political systems were a feature of both ancient Egypt and Mesopotamia, the way power was structured and rulership was conceived differed significantly, echoing their unique cultural and religious environments."

This approach will help you effectively answer SAQs and showcase your knowledge and analytical skills.

Sample Questions and Model Answers

1. *"Evaluate the influence of the Catholic Church in the evolution of education during the Middle Ages in Europe."*

Model Answer:

"The Catholic Church had a profound impact on the educational landscape of Middle Ages Europe. Notably, it established monastic schools, imparting education to monks and occasionally the local populace. These schools preserved and transmitted classical knowledge and religious texts through the copying and preservation of manuscripts. Further, the Church's advocacy of Latin as the scholarly language enabled a wider exchange of ideas and knowledge throughout Europe. During the later Middle Ages, the Church had a pivotal role in the inception of universities, evolving into hubs of higher learning and intellectual discourse. These institutions trained individuals in disciplines like theology, law, medicine, and the liberal arts, nurturing an intellectual and academic community. In conclusion, the Catholic Church was instrumental in the development of education during the Middle Ages in Europe by establishing monastic schools, promoting Latin as a scholarly language, and founding universities."

Explanation:

The model answer effectively addresses the sample question by analyzing the role of the Catholic Church in the development of education during the Middle Ages in Europe. The answer provides specific examples of the Church's contributions, such as establishing monastic schools, promoting Latin as the language of scholarship, and founding universities. The response highlights the broad historical context and captures the importance of the Catholic Church's contributions through well-organized paragraphs. The response uses relevant and specific instances to validate the claims regarding the Church's educational contributions.

2. *"Elucidate the triggers leading to the commencement of World War I."*

Model Answer:

"The outbreak of World War a complex interplay of political, economic, and social factors caused me. A significant cause was the intricate alliance systems developed amongst European nations. Alliances such as the Triple Entente and Triple Alliance fostered a complicated web of military commitments that escalated conflict once a country became engaged. An additional factor was the arms race among European nations, with countries bolstering their military capabilities in preparation for potential warfare. Nationalistic sentiments and imperialistic aspirations also stoked tensions amongst European powers as nations strived to assert their dominance and expand their territories. Although the immediate spark for World War I was the assassination of Archduke Franz Ferdinand of Austria-Hungary by a Serbian nationalist, the outbreak was a result of a confluence of factors, including alliance systems, imperialistic drives, and the arms race. These factors made it challenging to circumvent a larger-scale conflict. Thus, it's an oversimplification to attribute the onset of World War I solely to the assassination of Archduke Franz Ferdinand."

Explanation:

The exemplary response dissects the origins of World War I. The explanation effectively highlights how alliances, the arms race, nationalism, imperialist aspirations, and the assassination of Archduke Franz Ferdinand created an environment conducive to heightened tensions and warfare. The answer highlights the complexity of these causes and their role in triggering World War I. It also does an excellent job of explaining how these factors led to conflict through specific examples that link cause and effect.

EXCELLING IN THE DBQ (DOCUMENT-BASED QUESTION)

Mastering the Document-Based Question (DBQ) is critical for AP World History Exam success. As an essential component of the exam's Free Response section, the DBQ challenges students to analyze a variety of historical sources, develop a clear and defensible thesis statement, and use evidence effectively to construct a coherent argument. This guide will explore essential strategies and techniques for excelling in the DBQ.

Analyzing Primary Source Documents

The first step in mastering the DBQ is learning to analyze primary source documents effectively. These documents may include written texts, images, maps, or graphs. To analyze them successfully, follow these steps:

Example DBQ Prompt:

Assess the degree to which the Western societies underwent notable social, economic, and political transformations between 1750 and 1900 as a result of the Industrial Revolution.

Step 1: Read the Documents

Assume you have been provided with six primary source documents related to the Industrial Revolution. These documents may include political cartoons, excerpts from speeches, newspaper articles, letters, and photographs.

Step 2: Analyze Each Document
For each document, consider the following questions:

- What is the main idea or argument presented in the document?
- What is the author's purpose or perspective?
- What historical context influenced the document's creation?
- Are there any biases or limitations in the document?

Step 3: Categorize the Documents

Group the documents into categories based on their content, perspective, or theme. For example, you might have two documents discussing the economic changes brought about by the Industrial Revolution and three focusing on social changes.

Step 4: Extract Relevant Information

As you analyze each document, note any specific details, facts, or ideas relevant to the DBQ prompt. This information will be used as evidence to support your thesis statement and main points in your essay. Make sure to identify which document the information comes from, as you will need to reference it in your essay.

Step 5: Assess the Overall Picture

Once you have analyzed and categorized all the documents, assess their overall picture. Consider how the different perspectives or themes contribute to your understanding of the social, economic, and political changes that occurred during the Industrial Revolution.

Remember to consider any potential biases or limitations in the documents and acknowledge the different perspectives they present. This thorough analysis will strengthen your argument and demonstrate your ability to think critically and historically, setting you up for success on the exam.

Constructing a Strong Thesis Statement

A successful DBQ essay relies heavily on a strong thesis statement. It should be clear, concise, and directly address the prompt, offering a defensible position.

To create an effective thesis statement, follow these guidelines:

Step 1: Understand the Prompt

Make sure that you comprehend the DBQ prompt and its demands clearly. Interpret the main terms and concepts and consider various angles to approach the question.

For example, the prompt asks you to evaluate the extent to which the Industrial Revolution led to significant social, economic, and political changes in Western societies between 1750 and 1900. This implies a necessity to evaluate the influence exerted by the Industrial Revolution on these three societal domains, and ascertain the degree of these transformations.

Step 2: Develop your Position

Develop a position that directly addresses the prompt based on your analysis of the primary source documents and your understanding of the historical context. Make sure your position is defensible and supported by the evidence you've gathered from the documents.

Step 3: Craft a Clear and Concise Thesis Statement

Write a thesis statement that clearly communicates your position and the main points you will use to support it. Keep it concise, specific, and focused on the prompt.

For example, a strong thesis statement might be:

"The Industrial Revolution led to significant social, economic, and political changes in Western societies between 1750 and 1900, including the rise of urbanization, the growth of capitalist economies, and the emergence of labor movements, as evidenced by the primary source documents."

Constructing a Coherent Argument

Once you have a compelling thesis statement, you can begin constructing a coherent argument in your DBQ essay.

Follow these steps to achieve this:

Step 1: Outline Your Essay

It is recommended to create an outline for the essay, arranging the main points and evidence in a logical manner. Each paragraph should have a concise topic sentence that directly reinforces the thesis statement.

For example, your outline might look like this:

Introduction

- Introduce the topic and provide historical context
- Present your thesis statement

Body Paragraph

There is no set number of paragraphs for the DBQ (minimum or maximum.) Write as many paragraphs as you need to both use all seven documents and fully answer the prompt by developing the argument (and counter-argument if applicable) from your thesis, but each body paragraph will follow this general format:

- An assertion that encapsulates the primary argument of the section
- Analysis of the first document, including its main idea, author's perspective, and historical context
- Use evidence from the first document to support your argument
- Analysis of the second document, including its main idea, author's perspective, and historical context
- Use evidence from the second document to support your argument
- Explanation of how the documents relate to each other and contribute to your overall argument
- Possible counter-argument or acknowledgment of limitations/biases in the documents, if applicable

Repeat this format for additional body paragraphs, addressing different themes, perspectives, or categories of documents.

Conclusion

Summarize the main arguments presented in the paper and reiterate the thesis statement

Discuss the significance of your findings and their implications for the historical understanding of the Industrial Revolution

Step 2: Write Your Essay

Utilize your outline as a roadmap to compose a coherent, precise, and well-organized essay. During writing, it's crucial to ensure logical transitions between each paragraph, utilizing suitable transitional words and phrases to uphold consistency throughout the piece. Remember to refer to the primary source documents in your essay, using them as substantiation to back up your argument.

Example:

"The Industrial Revolution incited notable social, economic, and political modifications in Western societies between 1750 and 1900, encompassing the emergence of urbanization, the expansion of capitalist economies, and the birth of labor movements, as illustrated by the primary source documents.

Urbanization was a substantial societal shift triggered by the Industrial Revolution, as individuals relocated to cities seeking employment in factories. Document 1, a photograph of a bustling city street, illustrates the rapid growth of urban populations. The crowded conditions and the mix of people from different social classes suggest a shift in traditional societal structures. Document 2, a letter from a factory worker, describes the harsh living conditions in the city, highlighting the challenges faced by the working class during this period. Both documents reveal the impact of urbanization on social structures and living conditions in Western societies.

Economically, the Industrial Revolution led to the growth of capitalist economies, as demonstrated by Document 3, a graph showing the increase in global trade during this period. The broadening of trade networks and the surge in industrial production enabled wealth accumulation, reinforcing the supremacy of capitalist economies further. Document 4, a snippet from an economist's publication, proposes that the Industrial Revolution exacerbated economic disparities between the affluent and the impoverished. These documents demonstrate that the Industrial Revolution catalyzed the growth of capitalist economies and amplified the economic chasm within Western societies.

The Industrial Revolution also incited considerable political shifts, as labor movements sprung up in response to the novel social and economic conditions. Document 5, a political cartoon, depicts factory workers protesting for better working conditions and wages. This visual representation emphasizes the struggle for workers' rights during this period. Document 6, a speech by a labor leader, calls for political reforms to address the issues faced by the working class. Both documents highlight the political changes brought about by the Industrial Revolution, as workers began to mobilize and demand better treatment.

In conclusion, the Industrial Revolution profoundly impacted Western societies' social, economic, and political aspects between 1750 and 1900. The rise of urbanization, the growth of capitalist economies, and the emergence of labor movements all serve as evidence of these significant changes. By examining primary source documents, it is clear that the Industrial Revolution drastically altered the course of history, shaping the modern world we know today."

The essay summarizes the main points and restates the thesis statement, emphasizing the significance of the findings and their implications for understanding the historical context of the Industrial Revolution.

Step 3: Revise and Proofread

Once you've finished writing your essay, it's crucial to carefully review and edit your work in order to guarantee that it is properly structured, directly addresses the prompt, and provides strong evidence in support of your thesis statement. By revising and proofreading your DBQ essay, you will be able to present a coherent argument with a compelling central claim.

DBQs can be very challenging essays to write, but they do not have to be stressful. When you compose your essay, find an engaging thesis statement and support it with specific evidence from the documents. By following these steps and consistently practicing with sample DBQs, you will soon be able to prepare for the exam while developing valuable writing skills that can serve you well in the future.

Sample DBQs and Model Essays

DBQ Prompt 1:

Analyze the causes and consequences of the Green Revolution from the 1940s to the 1970s, and evaluate its impact on global food production and society.

Model Essay:

The Green Revolution, spanning from the 1940s to the 1970s, signifies a collection of research, development, and technology diffusion efforts intended to enhance global agricultural yield, especially in emerging economies. Spurred by anxieties about food deficits, malnutrition, and population expansion, the Green Revolution primarily brought high-yield varieties (HYV) of crops, chemical fertilizers and pesticides usage, and the adoption of contemporary irrigation methods. The aftermath of the Green Revolution included boosted worldwide food production, reduced starvation and malnutrition, alongside substantial socio-environmental impacts.

One of the primary triggers of the Green Revolution was the global worry about food availability and population surge, predominantly in developing countries. Post-World War II, numerous countries grappled with considerable food deficits due to war-associated devastation and swift population growth (Doc 1). The Ford Foundation and the Rockefeller Foundation, collaborating with local administrations and research institutions, recognized the necessity to counter these food deficits, initiating programs designed to formulate and distribute new agricultural technologies (Doc 2). These foundations likely aspired to reduce hunger and malnutrition while also advancing economic development and political stability in the developing world.

The integration of high-yielding varieties (HYV) of crops, such as wheat and rice, was a pivotal element in the triumph of the Green Revolution. Considerable enhancements in crop yields and agricultural productivity were accomplished through the research endeavors of institutions like the International Rice Research Institute and the International Maize and Wheat Improvement Center in developing new crop varieties (Doc 3). The creation of High Yielding Variety (HYV) crops, genetically altered to demonstrate positive reactions to chemical fertilizers and irrigation, allowed farmers to generate more food using the same land area.

The Green Revolution also saw the pervasive use of chemical fertilizers and pesticides contributing to elevated agricultural productivity. Farmers were urged to utilize these chemicals to augment soil fertility and control pests, leading to more abundant yields (Doc 4). Nevertheless, the heavy dependency on chemical inputs also led to adverse environmental consequences, like soil erosion, water contamination, and biodiversity loss (Doc 5). These environmental issues provoked concerns amongst scientists, activists, and the public, who advocated for more sustainable farming practices.

The Green Revolution resulted in several significant consequences, both beneficial and detrimental. Positively, there was a remarkable increase in global food production, alleviating hunger and malnutrition in many regions of the world (Doc 6). More abundant food availability also led to reduced food prices, making it more affordable for the impoverished (Doc 7). In addition, the farming sector experienced economic growth, as farmers could sell their excess crops in domestic and global markets.

Conversely, the Green Revolution also had social and environmental repercussions. The escalated use of machinery and modern farming methods often favored large-scale, affluent farmers, leading to a growing income disparity between wealthy and poor farmers (Doc 8). Small-scale farmers frequently could not afford the requisite inputs and technologies, resulting in their marginalization and, occasionally, expulsion from the land (Doc 9). Furthermore, the ecological consequences of the Green Revolution, such as soil exhaustion, water pollution, and loss of biodiversity, initiated a reevaluation of the long-term viability of these agricultural practices.

In summary, propelled by anxieties over food shortage and population surge, the Green Revolution led to the invention and widespread adoption of cutting-edge farming technologies, substantially boosting worldwide food output. While the Green Revolution aided in alleviating hunger and malnutrition and promoted economic expansion, it also caused considerable social and environmental consequences.

Explanation:

This composition meticulously evaluates the origins and repercussions of the Green Revolution, considering its influence on global food output and societal structures. Following a detailed overview of the historical context and the initiative's birth, the essay presents a comprehensive appraisal of both favorable and unfavorable outcomes. It adeptly assesses the impacts of different elements of the movement relative to each other and their broader implications on global food production and societal structures."

DBQ Prompt 2:

Examine the repercussions of colonialism on countries in Africa, Asia, and Latin America, focusing particularly on various forms of resistance that surfaced in opposition to colonial rule.

Model Essay:

The influence of colonialism on African, Asian, and Latin American countries was profound and enduring, molding their political, economic, and societal frameworks in diverse manners. Between the late 15th and early 20th centuries, European entities instated their dominance over these territories, capitalized on their resources, enforced their cultural norms and values, and substantially changed the existence of native communities. Colonialism's effects include not just political borders, economic dependencies, and cultural assimilation but also various forms of opposition against colonial subjugation.

An enduring consequence of colonialism is the arbitrary political borders instituted by European powers across Africa, Asia, and Latin America. During the Berlin Conference (1884-1885), European forces split Africa into zones of influence, drawing borders with disregard for the ethnic, linguistic, or cultural diversities among indigenous populations (Doc 1). Similarly, colonial powers set up administrative divisions in Asia and Latin America, often neglecting pre-existing political and cultural entities (Doc 2). These random boundaries continue to mold the political landscape of these regions, leading to ethnic tension, conflict, and struggles for national identity.

Another critical legacy of colonialism is the economic dependency of former colonies on their ex-colonizers. European powers exploited the resources and labor of their colonies, extracting raw materials for their industries and exporting finished goods back to the colonies (Doc 3). This system of economic exploitation generated a pattern of dependency on primary commodity export and manufactured goods import, which continues in many former colonies to this day (Doc 4). Economic systems established during the colonial era persist in shaping the developmental paths of these nations, frequently leading to underdevelopment, poverty, and disparity.

Colonialism also had enduring effects on the cultural panoramas of Africa, Asia, and Latin America. European powers sought to assimilate indigenous populations into their culture and values, often via education, religion, and language (Doc 5). Christian missionaries significantly influenced the cultural transformation of these regions, converting local populations to Christianity and introducing European languages, literature, and values (Doc 6). Despite certain elements of indigenous culture enduring and adjusting, the process of cultural integration and imposition of European values resulted in a multifaceted heritage influencing the cultural identities of these regions.

Diverse forms of resistance surfaced in Africa, Asia, and Latin America in opposition to colonial governance. Some native populations initiated armed revolts against colonial authorities, striving to reclaim their independence and conserve their way of life (Doc 7). Others adopted nonviolent resistance, like the Indian National Congress led by Mahatma Gandhi, which used nonviolent civil disobedience to demand independence from British rule (Doc 8). In certain cases, resistance manifested in the form of cultural conservation and rejuvenation, as native populations endeavored to retain and enhance their cultural identity amidst colonial dominance (Doc 9).

In summary, the persistent effects of colonialism on the nations of Africa, Asia, and Latin America are assorted and enduring. The random political boundaries, economic reliance, cultural integration, and various forms of resistance that originated during the colonial administration continue to mold the political, economic, and social terrains of these regions today. Understanding these legacies is paramount in addressing the challenges and prospects these countries face in the current era.

Explanation:

This essay scrutinizes the ramifications of colonialism on countries in Africa, Asia, and Latin America, emphasizing the different forms of resistance that arose to counter colonial domination. It probes into the political, economic, and cultural impacts of colonialism, shedding light on both the detrimental and transformative facets of European supremacy in these regions. The essay further investigates the assorted forms of resistance employed by native populations to defy colonial rule, underscoring the determination and resilience of these communities in the face of hardship. By delivering a comprehensive and nuanced analysis of colonial legacies, this essay illuminates the complex historical processes that persist in shaping the trajectories of these regions in the modern world.

TACKLING THE LEQ (LONG ESSAY QUESTION)

The Long Essay Question (LEQ) in World History is designed to evaluate your ability to explain and analyze significant historical issues while constructing a well-organized argument backed by evidence. When presented with the LEQ prompt, you'll be given a choice of three essay topics, each centered around the same theme and skill but set within distinct time periods.

The essay options are divided as follows:
- **Option 1:** 1200-1750
- **Option 2:** 1450-1900
- **Option 3:** 1750-2001

The writing section of the AP Exam consists of the Document-Based Question (DBQ) and the Long Essay Question (LEQ), with 40 minutes suggested for completing the latter. Within this timeframe, it is recommended to allocate 5 minutes for planning and 35 minutes for writing. This breakdown allows for effective time management and ensures that you can plan and write your essay within the allotted time.

How to Successfully Tackle the Long Essay Question (LEQ) in World History

Step 1: Understand The Prompt

Carefully read the given essay options and select the one that best aligns with your knowledge and interests.

For example, let's choose Option 2: 1450-1900, with the prompt:

"Analyze the factors that contributed to the growth of European overseas empires during the Age of Exploration."

The prompt asks you to analyze the factors that contributed to the growth of European overseas empires. This means that your essay should focus on examining the causes behind the expansion of European powers during the Age of Exploration. It uses the word **"analyze,"** which indicates that you should not only describe the factors but also examine their significance and explain how they contributed to the growth of European empires. This entails digging deeper into the causes and providing context for your arguments.

The prompt asks you to analyze the factors contributing to the growth of European empires, which implies that there could be several factors to discuss. Identifying these factors beforehand can help you organize your essay and ensure that your arguments are comprehensive and well-rounded. Possible subtopics for this prompt include technological advancements, economic motivations, and religious factors.

Take a few minutes to brainstorm what you know about that topic.

Step 2: Create an Outline

Prior to commencing your writing, formulate a concise outline to provide structure to your essay. This strategy ensures a logical and coherent flow to your essay, thereby enhancing the reader's comprehension of your points of argument.

Step 3: Write Your Essay

With a structural outline ready, begin drafting your essay. Employ clear and succinct language, steering clear of overly complicated sentences. Make your evidence and instances as specific as possible, and elaborate on their relevance to the prompt.

a. Introduction

Start by providing historical context for the Age of Exploration and European expansion. Then, present your thesis statement, which should directly address the prompt and outline the factors you will discuss in your essay.

For example:

"Throughout the Age of Exploration, spanning the 15th to the 17th century, European states initiated a series of journeys and conquests resulting in the formation of overseas empires. A fusion of technological progress, economic

incentives, and religious considerations propelled this expansion era. This essay will analyze how these factors contributed to the growth of European overseas empires, ultimately transforming the world order and global trade networks."

b. Body Paragraphs

Write a separate paragraph for each of the factors you identified in your outline. Every paragraph should initiate with a sentence that directly connects to the thesis. Subsequently, present specific evidence and examples to substantiate your arguments, such as technological advancements (for example, the caravel, compass, and astrolabe), economic motivations (like the quest for new trade routes and resources), and religious factors (like the propagation of Christianity). Analyze the importance of each aspect and elucidate how it fostered the growth of European overseas empires.

For example:

"The development of innovative navigational technologies was a significant factor in the expansion of European overseas empires. The highly maneuverable caravel allowed Europeans to sail across open seas easily and quickly. Additionally, the compass and astrolabe improved navigational accuracy, enabling sailors to determine their position and chart new courses more effectively. These technological advancements facilitated the exploration and conquest of new territories, laying the foundation for European imperial expansion.

Economic motivations also played a crucial role in the growth of European overseas empires. European powers sought to establish direct trade routes with Asia to bypass the costly and dangerous overland Silk Road controlled by Muslim empires. This desire for new trade routes led to the exploration of previously uncharted territories, such as the African coast and the Americas. The discovery of valuable resources, like gold, silver, and spices, further fueled European expansion as nations competed for control over these lucrative markets.

Religious factors also contributed to the growth of European overseas empires. The spread of Christianity was a significant driving force behind European expansion, as many explorers and conquistadors sought to convert indigenous populations to Christianity. This religious motivation often went hand in hand with political ambitions, as the spread of Christianity legitimized European claims to newly discovered territories and strengthened their influence in the global sphere."

As long as the essay adequately addresses the prompt, provides a clear and coherent argument, and is well-organized, the number of paragraphs in the body does not matter. The key is to ensure that each paragraph has a clear purpose, directly relates to the thesis statement, and contributes to the overall argument. Depending on the topic's complexity and the required depth of analysis, there may be more or fewer body paragraphs. Remember to use appropriate transitions and provide sufficient evidence and analysis for each point you discuss.

c. Conclusion

Connect your analysis back to the broader historical context and provide insights on the implications or long-term consequences of the factors you discussed.

For example:

"In conclusion, the growth of European overseas empires during the Age of Exploration was the result of a combination of technological advancements, economic motivations, and religious factors. These interconnected components empowered European nations to traverse unexplored territories, set up new trade pathways, and extend their global influence. The enlargement of European empires had a deep impact on world history, as it enabled the transfer of goods, ideologies, and cultures, consequently shaping the trajectory of human history."

Step 4: Proofread and Revise

Lastly, invest time in proofreading your essay for grammatical inaccuracies, ambiguous language, or inconsistencies in your points of argument. Confirm that your essay is orderly, concise, and understandable by implementing any required revisions.

Following these steps will prepare you to master the Long Essay Question (LEQ) in World History, demonstrating your ability to analyze historical issues and construct a well-organized, evidence-based argument.

Sample LEQs and Model Essays

LEQ Prompt 1:

Between 1750 and 1900, compare and contrast the political and economic impacts of European imperialism on two of the following regions: Africa, Asia, or Latin America.

Model Essay 1:

Between 1750 and 1900, European imperialism profoundly impacted various regions, including Africa and Asia. While both regions experienced significant political and economic changes as a result of imperialism, the nature and extent of these effects varied. This essay will compare and contrast European imperialism's political and economic effects on Africa and Asia, focusing on establishing European control, exploiting resources, and introducing new economic systems.

In both Africa and Asia, European imperialism led to the establishment of European control over vast territories. In Africa, the Scramble for Africa resulted in the partitioning of the continent among European powers, who imposed their political systems and borders on the indigenous populations. In Asia, European imperialism manifested differently, as some regions, such as India and Southeast Asia, fell under direct European control, while others, like China and Japan, experienced indirect influence or semi-colonial status. Despite these differences, European control disrupted traditional political structures and introduced new forms of governance in both regions.

European imperialism also led to the exploitation of resources in both Africa and Asia. European powers established extractive economies in these regions, extracting raw materials and exporting them to the metropoles. In Africa, resources such as rubber, gold, and diamonds were exploited, while in Asia, tea, opium, and spices were among the primary goods extracted. However, the extent of exploitation varied between the two regions, with Africa suffering more extensive resource depletion and environmental degradation.

Finally, European imperialism introduced new economic systems in both Africa and Asia. In Africa, European powers implemented the use of cash crops *and forced labor to meet the demands of the global market, disrupting traditional agricultural practices and causing food shortages. In Asia, European powers promoted the growth of plantation agriculture, mining, and manufacturing industries, which altered traditional economic structures and created new social and economic classes. However, the response to these new systems differed in each region, with Asia experiencing more significant economic growth and modernization due to European influence.*

In conclusion, European imperialism had both similar and divergent political and economic effects on Africa and Asia between 1750 and 1900. Although both regions experienced European control, resource exploitation, and the introduction of new economic systems, the extent and nature of these effects varied between the two regions. Understanding these differences provides insight into European imperialism's complex and varied consequences on the colonized regions during this period.

Explanation:

This model essay effectively addresses the prompt by comparing and contrasting European imperialism's political and economic effects on Africa and Asia. The essay begins with a clear introduction that outlines the main points to be discussed, followed by well-organized body paragraphs that explore each point in detail. The essay uses clear transitions to connect each point and demonstrate a strong, logical organization. The essay begins with the Scramble for Africa, first discussing European control over African territories, then resource exploitation and new economic systems. These points are then discussed in reverse order in the conclusion. Overall, this essay effectively demonstrates an understanding of European imperialism's political and economic effects in Africa and Asia between 1750–1900 and offers a nuanced comparison between these regions.

LEQ Prompt 2:

Investigate the similarities and differences in the strategies employed by revolutionary movements and their leaders to accomplish their objectives in two of the following revolutions between 1750 and 1900: the American Revolution, the French Revolution, and the Haitian Revolution.

Model Essay 2:

The American Revolution (1775-1783) and the Haitian Revolution (1791-1804) were two transformative episodes occurring between 1750 and 1900. Both upheavals strived for independence and the assertion of rights for their populations. This essay will dissect the similarities and disparities in how these revolutionary movements and their leaders chased their objectives, centering on the driving ideologies of the revolutions, the techniques utilized to fulfill their objectives, and the ultimate fallout of the revolutions.

A fundamental similarity between the American and Haitian Revolutions was the influence of Enlightenment philosophies on their ideological basis. Both movements were spurred by a quest for liberty, equality, and self-determination. The American Revolution took significant cues from the works of Enlightenment thinkers such as John Locke and Montesquieu, who championed innate rights and power separation. In contrast, the Haitian Revolution was kindled by the French Revolution and its focus on human rights, along with the wider principles of the Enlightenment. However, the Haitian Revolution underscored the abolition of slavery and racial equality, while the American Revolution sought primarily political independence from Britain.

Another similarity between the American and Haitian Revolutions was the use of armed conflict to achieve their goals. Both revolutions involved violent struggles against their respective colonial powers. The American Revolution witnessed the Thirteen Colonies opposing British dominion, ultimately leading to the birth of the United States. In comparison, the Haitian Revolution involved a large-scale insurrection of enslaved people against French colonial authority, leading to the creation of an independent Haiti. Nevertheless, the conflict dynamics differed substantially, with the American Revolution primarily being a conflict between structured armies, while the Haitian Revolution was characterized by guerrilla warfare and widespread uprisings among enslaved people.

Finally, while both the American and Haitian Revolutions attained independence from their respective colonial powers, their outcomes varied in terms of social and political implications. The American Revolution resulted in the formation of a democratic republic that included a constitution safeguarding specific individual freedoms, although it initially allowed for the continuation of slavery. In contrast, the Haitian Revolution led to the establishment of the first-ever republic governed by individuals of African descent and the complete eradication of slavery. Despite these accomplishments, both countries encountered ongoing struggles in fulfilling their revolutionary ideals, with the United States grappling with matters related to slavery and civil rights, and Haiti confronting political instability and economic challenges.

In conclusion, the American and Haitian Revolutions shared similarities in their ideological foundations and methods of achieving their goals but differed in their ultimate outcomes and long-term consequences. Both revolutions were influenced by Enlightenment ideas and involved armed conflict against their respective colonial powers. However, their outcomes diverged in terms of their social and political consequences, reflecting the distinct contexts and aspirations of the two revolutionary movements. By analyzing these similarities and differences, we can better understand the complex dynamics and lasting legacies of these transformative events in world history.

Explanation:

This essay effectively explores the similarities and differences between revolutionary movements in the United States, Haiti, and France between 1750 and 1900. The essay begins by clearly explaining the two colonies included in the prompt and then explaining each colony's background and primary goal. The essay then examines how these colonies adopted radical ideas, such as Enlightenment ideas from Europe, central to their ideological foundations. This is followed by a strong conclusion outlining both revolutions' similarities and differences. Overall, this essay successfully demonstrates an understanding of these revolutions' critical political and economic effects on Africa, Asia, and Europe during this period.

COMPREHENSIVE CONTENT REVIEW

Unit 1: The Global Tapestry (1200 - 1450)

1. Emergence of New States and Empires

This epoch was marked by the emergence of mighty empires and states that greatly influenced the trajectory of human civilization.

- In the Far East, the Yuan Dynasty, steered by the Mongols, supplanted the Song Dynasty, later making way for the Ming Dynasty. These dynastic shifts brought forth substantial cultural, political, and economic evolution. For example, the Song Dynasty is known for its advancements in science and technology, whereas the Ming Dynasty saw the expeditions of Zheng He, symbolizing the empire's naval might and intent for global diplomacy.
- In India, the Delhi Sultanate rose to prominence as a significant hub of Islamic culture and governance. The Delhi Sultanate rulers were proficient in unifying vast regions of the Indian subcontinent under a central political system.
- The Mali Empire ascended as one of the most impactful states in West Africa. Its wealth was grounded in the gold and salt trade. Mansa Musa, one of its rulers, was particularly famous for his extravagant pilgrimage to Mecca, which put Mali on the map for European and Middle Eastern states.

2. Cultural Developments and Interactions

The diffusion and intermingling of diverse cultural practices, philosophical systems, and religious beliefs continued to shape societies globally.

- Religions and philosophies like Buddhism, Christianity, Islam, and Confucianism expanded, impacting broad regions and a multitude of cultures.
- The emergence of vernacular languages triggered an intellectual and literary surge. Dante Alighieri's "Divine Comedy," written in the Tuscan dialect of Italian, Geoffrey Chaucer's "Canterbury Tales" in Middle English, and the poetic works of Chinese literati in vernacular language are some notable examples.

3. Economic Systems

Trade networks expanded and became more sophisticated during this era.

- The Silk Road remained an important conduit for goods and cultural exchange, particularly during the Pax Mongolica, when the Mongol Empire's control enhanced safety and stability along the route.
- The Indian Ocean trade network linked East Africa, Arabia, India, Southeast Asia, and China, fostering exchange of goods like spices, textiles, and precious stones.
- The Trans-Saharan trade network connected West Africa with North Africa and the Mediterranean world, primarily facilitating the trade of gold, salt, and slaves.

4. Social Structures

Societies of this era were often organized in hierarchical structures.

- In Europe, feudalism emerged as a dominant system, with power hierarchically divided among kings, nobles, knights, and serfs.
- In India, the caste system provided a rigid social structure, defining one's profession, social status, and rules for interaction and marriage.
- In other regions like West Africa and the Americas, social structures were often more fluid and could change with the rise and fall of different clans or empires.

Unit 2: Networks of Exchange (1200 - 1450)

1. Growth of Trade Networks

Trade networks saw considerable expansion and growth during this period, driven by several political, economic, and technological factors.

- The Mongol Empire, covering a vast area of Eurasia, was instrumental in protecting and facilitating trade routes. This period, commonly known as the Pax Mongolica, fostered increased trade and cultural interchange across Asia, Europe, and Africa.
- The Indian Ocean trade network flourished due to advancements in maritime technology and the collective efforts of diverse maritime societies. Major goods exchanged included spices from the Southeast

Asian 'Spice Islands', Chinese silk and porcelain, Indian textiles, and Arabian incense.

- In the Americas, the Mississippians in the east and the Pueblo people in the west built significant trade networks. The Mississippian city of Cahokia was a significant trade hub, connecting various regional cultures and economies.

2. Spread of Cultural, Religious, and Scientific Knowledge

As trade networks expanded, they not only facilitated the exchange of goods, but also ideas, technologies, and cultural practices.

- The spread of Islam was significantly impacted by these expanding trade networks. Traders, scholars, and Sufi missionaries traveled these routes, bringing Islamic practices and beliefs to new regions like Sub-Saharan Africa, South Asia, and Southeast Asia.
- Along the Silk Roads, the interaction of different cultures led to a vibrant exchange of ideas, art, and science. Chinese inventions like papermaking, printing, gunpowder, and the compass reached the West, while India's numeral system and various scientific and philosophical ideas flowed both East and West.

3. Technological Innovations

Technology played a crucial role in enabling and enhancing these exchanges.

- The use of the compass, an invention acquired from China, greatly improved maritime navigation. It was complemented by improvements in shipbuilding, including the development of the Arab dhow and Chinese junk, enabling more effective exploration and trade.
- Innovations in cartography, like the production of more accurate maps and sea charts, facilitated the work of traders and explorers. The astrolabe, an instrument used for navigation, was improved upon by Muslim scholars and widely used in sea travel.
- New techniques in papermaking and book production, combined with the invention of the movable type printing press in China, led to increased literacy and the wider dissemination of knowledge.

4. Environmental Consequences

The expansion of trade and the growth of cities also had environmental impacts.

- Intensified agriculture, often to produce goods for trade, led to deforestation and other forms of environmental degradation.
- Overfishing in certain maritime regions occurred due to increasing demand for fish as a food source in growing urban areas.
- The spread of diseases along trade routes also had significant impacts on human populations. For example, the Bubonic Plague (Black Death) spread along the Silk Road, devastating populations across Eurasia.

Unit 3: Land-Based Empires (1450 - 1750)

1. Rise and Expansion of Empires

In this age, numerous influential empires ascended, wielding considerable sway over world history.

- The Ottoman Empire emerged as a powerful state straddling Europe, Asia, and Africa, ruling over diverse religious and ethnic groups. This empire utilized an administrative system known as the devshirme, where Christian boys from the empire's European territories were taken, converted to Islam, and trained for civil administration or military service (Janissaries).
- The Qing Dynasty in China implemented a bureaucracy based on the Confucian civil service examination system, allowing the empire to effectively govern its vast and diverse population. Meanwhile, in Russia, the Tsar centralized power and expanded territory, creating a multinational, multiethnic empire.

2. Political Systems and State Administration

Each empire had its distinct approach to governance and state administration, which played a significant role in their growth and stability.

- Bureaucratic structures were a common feature, providing an organizational framework for these vast empires. Many of them, including the Ottomans with their Devshirme system and the Chinese with their Civil Service Exam, had unique ways of recruiting and training officials.
- Absolute rule was a common feature in many European states. Monarchs claimed divine right to rule and centralized power in their hands, often in conflict with other elements of society, such as the nobility or the clergy.

3. Cultural Developments and Interactions

Cultural and intellectual exchange continued to flourish during this period, often sponsored by the state.

- The Ottoman Empire experienced a fusion of Persian, Turkic, and Arab traditions, influencing its literature, art, and architecture, evident in structures like the Suleymaniye Mosque in Istanbul.
- The Mughal Empire saw a convergence of Persianate and Indian cultures, prompting new developments in literature, music, and visual arts.
- In China, literature and arts thrived, with notable developments in novel-writing and porcelain production.

4. Social Structures and Economic Systems

As these empires expanded and consolidated, social hierarchies were reinforced, and economic systems evolved.

- Many societies maintained strict social hierarchies. In Europe, the remnants of feudalism slowly gave way to a more centralized structure under monarchies. In India, the caste system continued to dictate social interactions.
- Economically, mercantilism became an important policy in many European states, influencing the era of exploration and colonialism. In Asia, a flourishing of trade and urbanization occurred under the peace and stability provided by the major empires.

Unit 4: Transoceanic Interconnections (1450 - 1750)

1. Age of Exploration

This era marked the advent of sustained, direct interaction between previously isolated world regions, largely driven by European maritime exploration.

- The Portuguese and Spanish, led by explorers such as Vasco da Gama and Christopher Columbus, pioneered these voyages in search of trade routes to Asia, and subsequently, for colonial territories.
- The subsequent explorations by other European powers, including the English, Dutch, and French, led to the mapping of the globe's major landmasses and oceans.

2. Columbian Exchange

This term describes the exchange of goods, ideas, people, and diseases between the New and Old Worlds that began after Columbus's voyages.

- New World crops such as corn (maize), potatoes, tomatoes, and cocoa had a transformative impact on the Old World, significantly changing diets and supporting population growth.
- Conversely, Old World animals like horses, pigs, and cattle dramatically transformed societies and ecosystems in the Americas.
- The exchange also included forced migration of enslaved Africans to the Americas, resulting in significant demographic, social, and cultural changes.
- Diseases brought from the Old World, such as smallpox, devastated indigenous populations in the Americas.

3. Emergence of European Dominance

European maritime powers established trade networks and colonies across the world.

- In the Americas, colonies were established by the Spanish, Portuguese, English, French, and Dutch. These colonies extracted valuable resources and wealth, often exploiting native populations and enslaved Africans.
- In Asia, Europeans established trading post empires. The Portuguese controlled strategic ports around the Indian Ocean, while the Dutch established control in Indonesia, and the British began their presence in India.
- The competition for trade and colonies led to conflicts among European powers, shaping the dynamics of European politics and alliances.

4. Transformation of Societies

The increased global interactions led to transformative social, cultural, and political changes in societies.

- The Atlantic Slave Trade led to horrific depopulation in certain regions of Africa, but also led to cultural diffusion and the creation of new African diaspora communities in the Americas.
- Syncretic religions, such as Vodou in Haiti and Santería in Cuba, developed as a fusion of traditional African religions with Christianity.

- The encounter with the New World and its people challenged and changed European philosophical and scientific thought, contributing to intellectual movements like the Enlightenment.

Unit 5: Revolutions (1750 - 1900)

1. Transformation in Political Landscape

This epoch experienced several political revolutions that significantly altered global political formations.

- The American Revolution resulted in the establishment of a new state founded on republican ideologies and the notion of individual liberties. Its impact was far-reaching, inciting movements for self-determination and democracy globally.
- The French Revolution, fueled by Enlightenment ideologies, drastically transformed French societal and political structures. The principles of liberty, equity, and fraternity that originated in France reverberated across borders, shaping political developments in multiple parts of Europe and the Americas.
- The Haitian Revolution (1791-1804) was a victorious uprising by enslaved individuals, culminating in Haiti's establishment as a free, sovereign republic, effectively challenging entrenched social and racial hierarchies.

2. Industrial Revolution

This period witnessed speedy industrialization, primarily in Europe and North America, bringing dramatic alterations to economies and societies.

- The creation and diffusion of new technologies and machinery, like the steam engine, the spinning jenny, and the power loom, brought a revolution in production in industries such as textiles and iron.
- Industrialization led to urbanization, as people moved to cities in search of work, dramatically transforming demographics and living conditions.
- Industrial capitalism became the dominant economic system, with entrepreneurs investing in factories and infrastructure to generate profit.

3. Nationalism and Imperialism

Rising sentiments of nationalism led to the unification and expansion of states, while the industrial powers engaged in imperialism.

- Nationalism resulted in the unification of Italy and Germany, disrupting the power equilibrium in Europe.
- The "Scramble for Africa" witnessed European powers colonizing most of the African continent and exploiting its resources for industrial production.
- The Opium Wars and the "Unequal Treaties" resulted in significant territorial and economic concessions from China to Western powers and Japan.

4. Societal Reforms and Movements

The political and industrial revolutions ignited a variety of societal reform movements and alterations in social structures.

- Philosophies such as socialism and communism surfaced as critiques of capitalism and the industrialized society. These philosophies inspired various labor movements and reforms aimed at improving conditions for the working-class population.
- Feminist movements advanced, championing for women's rights, including the right to vote. Personalities like Mary Wollstonecraft in Britain advocated for enhanced gender equality.
- The movement to abolish the trans-Atlantic slave trade and slavery made significant progress, resulting in the prohibition of the slave trade and the ultimate abolition of slavery in numerous parts of the globe.

Unit 6: Industrialization's Effects (1750 to 1900)

1. Economic Shifts

Industrialization significantly changed global economic structures and practices.

- The factory system and mechanized production led to mass production, making goods more affordable and accessible, but also resulted in labor exploitation and subpar working conditions.
- The invention of railroads, steamships, and telegraph lines greatly enhanced transportation and communication, promoting global trade and exchange.

- The rise of industrial capitalism led to wealth accumulation and middle-class expansion in industrialized societies while also intensifying social inequalities.

2. Imperialism and Global Trade

The Industrial Revolution drove European imperialism as industrializing nations sought raw materials for factories and markets for their goods.

- The "Scramble for Africa" saw virtually all of Africa divided among European powers. The imposition of European rule had profound impacts on African societies and economies.
- In Asia, the British East India Company's control over India increased, transforming its economy and integrating it into the global trade network as a major supplier of raw materials and a market for British goods.
- China and Japan had differing responses to Western imperialism. China's resistance led to wars and unequal treaties that compromised its sovereignty, while Japan's Meiji Restoration modernized and industrialized the country, enabling it to resist Western domination and become a colonial power itself.

3. Social Changes

Industrialization brought significant social changes and challenges.

- Urbanization accelerated, but rapid growth often led to overcrowded cities with poor living conditions. This period also saw advancements in public health and sanitation in response to these conditions.
- The factory system led to a fundamental shift in labor patterns. Workers often experienced long hours, low pay, and unsafe conditions, leading to the growth of labor unions and movements for labor rights.
- Industrialization influenced gender roles and family structures. Numerous women and children toiled in factories under harsh conditions. However, the rising middle class began to espouse the "cult of domesticity," highlighting women's roles within the domestic sphere.

4. Ideological Reactions

Industrialization provoked diverse ideological responses and adaptations.

- Karl Marx and Friedrich Engels' works critiqued the intrinsic inequalities within capitalism and called for a worker-led revolution to establish a socialist society.
- Movements for social reform surfaced, advocating for changes in labor rights, women's suffrage, and education. The abolitionist movement gained substantial traction in the United States and the British Empire.
- Social Darwinism, a skewed interpretation of Charles Darwin's theories, was utilized to rationalize racial hierarchy and imperial supremacy.

Unit 7: Worldwide Confrontations (1900 - Present)

1. World Wars

The initial half of the twentieth century witnessed two world wars, causing unparalleled devastation and reshaping international relations.

- The complexities of alliances, disputes, and stress points among European nations led to World War I from 1914 to 1918. This war triggered significant political shifts, marking the end of several empires and the inception of new nations.
- The onset of World War II (1939 - 1945) was triggered by fascist hostilities in Europe and Asia. The confrontation escalated on a global scale, with increased fatalities and the horrific Holocaust. The conflict culminated with the deployment of atomic weapons on Japan, ushering in the nuclear era.

2. The Cold War

Post World War II, global ideologies split the world, sparking an extended Cold War between the U.S.-led capitalist West and the Soviet Union-led communist East.

- Political and military tension, proxy wars, an arms race, and a space race characterized this time period. Despite escalating tensions, the two superpowers averted direct military engagement. The Cold War witnessed numerous African, Asian, and Caribbean nations securing independence from European colonial powers. The newly independent states often became arenas for ideological influence between the United States and the Soviet Union.

3. Wave of Decolonization and Independence Movements

The fallout of World War II also ushered in a wave of decolonization and movements for independence.

- India achieved independence from British rule in 1947, following an extensive nonviolent resistance movement championed by Mahatma Gandhi among others.
- Numerous African nations obtained independence in the 1950s and 60s, often subsequent to considerable opposition against European powers.
- The establishment of new nations frequently led to disputes over borders, resources, and political supremacy, the impacts of which persist in the present day.

4. Ongoing Conflicts and Challenges

Despite advancements, the world continues to grapple with conflicts and challenges.

- Various regions worldwide continue to grapple with issues such as ethno-nationalist conflicts, religious radicalism, and resource-centric wars.
- Global predicaments like climate change, pandemics, and refugee crises necessitate a collaborative international approach.

Unit 8: Cold War and Decolonization (1945 - 1989)

1. The Cold War

The epoch was dominated by fierce geopolitical rivalry between two prevailing forces, the United States and the Soviet Union, along with their corresponding allies.

- The philosophical dichotomy between capitalism (championed by the U.S. and its Western allies) and communism (supported by the Soviet Union and the Eastern Bloc) was a pivotal aspect of the Cold War.
- While the U.S. and the Soviet Union steered clear of direct warfare, conflicts often manifested via surrogate engagements, like the Korean War (1950 - 1953) and the Vietnam War (1955 - 1975), where they supported contrasting sides.
- The nuclear arms competition and the prospect of Mutually Assured Destruction (MAD) restricted direct confrontation but amplified worldwide tension and apprehension.

- The space rivalry, an extension of the overarching Cold War competition, facilitated substantial scientific and technological progress, most notably the lunar landing by the U.S. in 1969.

2. Colonialism's End and the Rise of New Nations

This era witnessed the downfall of European colonial empires and the birth of newly independent nations, especially across Africa and Asia.

- Numerous factors like the weakened state of European powers post-World War II, growing nationalist movements within colonies, and international anti-colonialism pressure facilitated decolonization.
- The decolonization process often ushered in political instability, economic challenges, and conflict. In many instances, the legacy of arbitrarily drawn colonial borders led to ethnic and tribal conflicts.
- Newly independent nations navigated the complexities of the Cold War, aligning with either the US or Soviet Union, or striving to remain non-aligned, as evident in the Non-Aligned Movement.

3. Changes in Society and Culture

This period also witnessed substantial social and cultural transformations.

- The latter half of the 20th century observed a wave of social change, including the Civil Rights Movement in the US, the Feminist Movement, and anti-war demonstrations. These movements aimed to challenge social norms and inequality, seeking broader civil liberties and political rights.
- Global cultural exchange increased, driven by advances in technology and media. This period witnessed the growth of a global culture, influenced by Western, and particularly American, media and lifestyle.
- However, this era also saw resistance to cultural homogenization and efforts to preserve indigenous and local cultures.

Unit 9: The Age of Global Interconnectedness (Post-1989 to Now)

1. The Cold War's Consequences and the Evolution of the Global Scenario

The dissolution of the Soviet Union in 1991 signified the end of the Cold War epoch, leaving the United States as the unrivaled global superpower.

- This transition fostered the spread of principles related to liberal democracy and the free-market economic system. Despite this, the transition was met with numerous hurdles, especially in Eastern Europe and Central Asia, as they navigated the intricacies of this metamorphosis.
- Interestingly, China managed to incorporate aspects of capitalist economics while preserving its one-party governance, propelling its growth as an influential entity in global commerce.

2. Progress in Technology and Economic Convergence

The twilight of the 20th and dawn of the 21st centuries observed extraordinary advancements in technology that expedited the phenomenon of globalization.

- Developments in information and communication technologies, for instance, the internet and mobile devices, have transformed the face of global communication, while improvements in logistics have boosted the scale of international commerce.
- Global trade accords and institutions, such as the World Trade Organization (WTO), have catalyzed the growing interconnection of the worldwide economy. This era also saw the emergence of global business entities.

3. Social Shifts and Cultural Interactions
The phenomenon of globalization has spurred significant societal transformations and heightened the level of cross-cultural exchanges.

- The influx of people across national borders has amplified, resulting in increasingly diverse societies. Nevertheless, this has led to associated complications, such as the drain of skilled personnel and xenophobic attitudes.
- English has gained stature as an international lingua franca, and Western, notably American, cultural influences have seeped into various corners of the globe. There have been concerns about the possible homogenization of global cultures.
- The worldwide adoption of certain lifestyle trends and dietary customs has made significant health impacts, resulting in the rise of non-communicable diseases like obesity and diabetes globally.

4. Universal Challenges

The age of globalization has brought to light several global dilemmas that require coordinated responses.

- Climate change, largely induced by industrial activities and deforestation, has ascended as a crucial worldwide concern. As a countermeasure, global initiatives such as the Paris Agreement aim to curb greenhouse gas emissions.
- Other urgent issues include worldwide inequality, disease outbreaks, international acts of terrorism, and threats to cybersecurity.

5. Counteracting the Detrimental Outcomes of Globalization

Various forms of opposition have surfaced to combat the unfavorable outcomes of globalization.

- Anti-globalization rallies have manifested in response to perceived injustices within the global financial structure, notably seen during protests at WTO conventions.
- In certain regions, nationalist inclinations have seen a revival, often as a backlash against perceived dangers that globalization poses to national identities or economies.

EFFECTIVE WAYS TO STUDY AND TOOLS TO USE

To thrive in the AP World History examination, it's imperative to employ potent learning strategies and resources.

The following strategies can greatly help you in your preparation:

1. Creating a Study Plan and Schedule

A well-structured study plan is essential for success in any exam.

To create an effective study plan for AP World History, consider the following steps:

Step 1: Assess Your Current Knowledge

Before creating your study plan, take a diagnostic test or review the syllabus to determine your strengths and weaknesses. This will help you understand which topics or historical periods need more focus and time. For example, if you need help understanding the political dynamics of the early modern period, dedicate more time to that area of study.

Step 2: Set Specific Goals

Establish both immediate and long-range objectives for your study routine. An immediate objective could be to tackle a specific section or subject within a week, while a long-range objective could be to cover an entire historical period or theme over a month.

Step 3: Allocate Time Wisely

Create a schedule that balances your AP World History studies with other academic commitments and extracurricular activities. For example, you could dedicate one hour every weekday and two hours on weekends to studying AP World History. Make sure to allocate time for reviewing and practicing exam questions, too.

Sample Weekly Schedule:
- **Monday:** 1 hour - Unit 1: The Global Tapestry
- **Tuesday:** 1 hour - Unit 2: Networks of Exchange
- **Wednesday:** 1 hour - Unit 3: Land-Based Empires
- **Thursday:** 2 hours - Unit 4: Transoceanic Interconnections and Unit 5: Revolutions
- **Friday:** 1 hour - Review of the week's material and practice questions
- **Saturday:** 2 hours - Unit 6: Consequences of Industrialization and Unit 7: Global Conflict
- **Sunday:** 2 hours - Unit 8: Global Conflict and Unit 9: Globalization

Step 4: Stick to The Schedule

Consistency is the cornerstone of achievement. Establish a routine and follow your study schedule diligently. Use a planner, calendar, or digital app to track your progress and hold yourself accountable.

Creating and sticking to a study plan will set you up for success in the AP World History exam.

2. Utilizing Flashcards, Mnemonics, and Other Memory Aids

The AP World History exam is a test of your retention, knowledge, and ability to understand historical concepts and trends. To ensure the retention of the knowledge you've accumulated in class, it's crucial to utilize resources like flashcards, memory aids, and other tools that encourage learning via repetition.

a. Flashcards

Flashcards are a useful tool for memorizing key terms, events, and concepts. They help reinforce your memory through active recall, where you must retrieve the information from your memory rather than passively review it.

Example:

Front: "Feudalism"

Back: *"A socio-political and economic structure dominant in medieval Europe, marked by a tier of lords and vassals who rendered military and other services in return for land and safeguarding."*

To use flashcards effectively, you can follow these tips:
- Create flashcards for important terms, events, people, and concepts.
- Use both physical flashcards or digital platforms like Quizlet or Anki, which allow for spaced repetition, a proven learning technique.
- Regularly review your flashcards, starting with the most challenging ones.
- Gradually increase the time intervals between reviews as you become more confident with the material.

b. Mnemonics

Mnemonic devices are memory techniques that help you remember complex information more easily. They can be particularly helpful in AP World History for remembering dates, sequences of events, or key concepts.

Here are a few types of memory aids:

Acronyms

Construct a word or phrase using the initial letters of the items you're aiming to memorize.

Example:

To remember the major causes of World War I, you can use the acronym "MAIN":
- Militarism
- Alliances
- Imperialism
- Nationalism

Rhymes

Use rhymes or simple poems to remember information.

Example:

To remember the Great Depression in the US, you can use a simple poem:

"Too much stock, too little cash/Great Depression (of) 1929."

Stories or Visual Images

Stories or images help you remember concepts in AP World History. For example, if prompting for the causes of independence movements in Latin America, you could envision a donkey in an aguardiente distillery (sugar cane alcohol) with powder kegs stacked around it. The powder kegs represent Spain, and the donkey represents Spanish rule. You can use this image to help you recall that Spain's economic mismanagement contributed to Latin American independence movements.

Mnemonics are effective study tools that can help you learn and remember important concepts, events, and people in AP World History.

c. Mind Maps And Timelines

Visual aids, such as mind maps and timelines, can help you understand and remember the relationships between events and concepts by displaying them in a graphical format.

Example:

Create a mind map to illustrate the causes and effects of the French Revolution:

Central node: French Revolution

Causes:
- Financial crisis
- Enlightenment ideas
- Social inequality

Effects:
- Rise of Napoleon
- Spread of nationalism
- Influence on future revolutions

To use mind maps and timelines effectively:

• Organize information hierarchically or chronologically, depending on the topic.
• Use color coding or symbols to distinguish between different categories or themes.
• Review and update your visual aids as you learn new information.

• By incorporating flashcards, mnemonics, and other memory aids into your AP World History study routine, you can enhance your memory retention and recall, making it easier to master the vast amount of information required for the exam.

3. Take Advantage of Online Resources and Study Groups

Taking advantage of online resources and study groups can greatly enhance your understanding and retention of the AP World History material. Collaborative learning and online resources can provide different perspectives, improve problem-solving skills, and offer additional support during your exam preparation.

a. Online Resources

The internet offers a wealth of resources to help you study AP World History effectively.

Here are some examples and how they can help:

a. Khan Academy (https://www.khanacademy.org/humanities/ap-world-history)

Khan Academy offers comprehensive video lessons and articles on AP World History topics. These resources help clarify concepts and provide in-depth explanations that complement your textbook.

b. Crash Course World History (https://www.youtube.com/playlist?list=PLBDA2E52FB1EF80C9)

This YouTube series by John Green provides engaging and concise overviews of key historical periods and themes. These videos can serve as a helpful supplement to your reading and make complex ideas more accessible.

c. College Board (https://apstudents.collegeboard.org/courses/ap-world-history-modern)

The College Board's official AP World History course and exam information includes a comprehensive course description, sample exam questions, and scoring guidelines. Familiarize yourself with these resources to understand the exam format and expectations.

b. Study Groups

Forming or joining study groups with classmates or peers can promote a collaborative learning environment where you can:

- **Discuss Topics**

Engaging in conversations about key concepts, historical events, or themes can deepen your understanding and expose you to different perspectives.

- **Share Resources**

Exchange study materials, such as notes, flashcards, or online resources, to access a wider range of information and study techniques.

- **Quiz Each Other**

Test each other's knowledge by asking questions or conducting mock exams. This can help you identify improvement areas and enhance your active recall abilities.

- **Stay Motivated**

Encourage and support each other throughout the exam preparation process, making it easier to maintain focus and motivation.

Example:

Create a weekly study group meeting agenda:
- **Week 1:** Discuss the causes and effects of the French Revolution.
- **Week 2:** Compare and contrast the political systems of ancient Rome and Han China.
- **Week 3:** Analyze the impact of the Columbian Exchange on global trade and cultural exchange.
- **Week 4:** Review Period 3: Regional and Transregional Interactions (c. 600 CE to c. 1450) and conduct a mock exam.

By taking advantage of online resources and study groups, you can access diverse learning materials, develop a deeper understanding of AP World History content, and stay motivated throughout your exam preparation journey.

By adopting these strategies, you can maximize your chances of success in the AP World History exam and develop a strong foundation for future academic endeavors in the field of history.

TEST DAY STRATEGIES AND TIPS

To perform well on the AP World History exam, it's crucial to approach test day with effective strategies and tips that can help ensure success. The following suggestions can help you prepare mentally and physically, manage stress and anxiety, and make the most of your time during the test.

Prepare Mentally and Physically for the Exam

Preparing mentally and physically for the AP World History exam is crucial for optimal performance on test day. By attending to your physical and mental wellbeing, you're ensuring that you can maintain focus, retrieve information, and manage stress during the examination.

Here are some more insights and examples on how to prepare both mentally and physically:

- **Develop a Consistent Sleep Schedule**

For exam readiness, it is best to keep a regular sleep schedule in the weeks before the test. This means keeping a regular sleep-wake cycle every day. Maintaining a consistent sleep cycle aids in the regulation of your body's natural rhythm, ensuring you are adequately rejuvenated for the examination. The general consensus among professionals is that an ideal night's sleep spans between seven and nine hours.

- **Engage in Light Exercise**

Incorporating physical activity into your everyday schedule assists in mitigating stress levels, enhancing mental clarity, and bolstering general health. Prior to the examination, engage in light physical activities such as strolling, running, or practicing yoga to optimize your physical and cognitive state.

Allocate 30 minutes of your day to walking, opt for a morning jog, or participate in evening yoga sessions to alleviate stress and sustain optimal physical and mental health.

- **Practice Mindfulness and Relaxation Techniques**

Adopt a mindfulness routine or master relaxation techniques to calm your mind and improve focus. Techniques such as guided visualization, progressive muscle tension release, and deep respiration have demonstrated effectiveness in minimizing anxiety and amplifying mental preparedness.

Dedicate a daily slot of 10–15 minutes for deep respiration exercises. These involve inhaling deeply for a count of four, holding your breath for the same duration, and exhaling for another four counts.

- **Simulate Exam Conditions**

Familiarize yourself with the exam format and conditions by taking practice tests under timed conditions. By acquainting yourself with the test environment and building your mental endurance, you can better prepare yourself for the exam.

For instance, set a timer and take a full-length practice test in a quiet, distraction-free environment to simulate the actual test day experience.

- **Visualize Success**

Use positive visualization techniques to imagine yourself performing well on the exam. This can help build confidence and reduce anxiety. Devote a small amount of time daily to envision yourself taking the exam with ease, easily recalling information, and answering questions with confidence.

- **Create a Pre-exam Checklist**

Create a list of items you'll need for the exam, like your ID, pencils, erasers, and a water bottle. Having everything arranged and ready beforehand can reduce stress and make you feel more prepared.

- **Stay Hydrated**

It's crucial to make sure your body stays hydrated in the days before the exam by drinking lots of water. Your ability to focus and think clearly can be affected by dehydration.

By following these tips and examples, you can effectively mentally and physically prepare for the AP World History exam, increasing your chances of success on test day.

Manage Stress and Anxiety

Managing stress and anxiety is critical for success on the AP World History exam, as excess stress can negatively impact concentration, memory, and decision-making.

Here are more insights and procedures on how to effectively manage stress and anxiety:

- **Know What Stress and Anxiety Look Like**

Develop the ability to identify the physiological and emotional indicators of stress and anxiety. These may include an accelerated heart rate, superficial breathing, muscular tension, irritability, or difficulties in focusing. Recognizing these signs early on allows for timely intervention before they escalate.

- **Practice Grounding Techniques**

Grounding techniques can help you stay focused and calm in stressful situations. Some methods include:

    a. **5-4-3-2-1 Technique:** This strategy can be carried out by noticing five visible objects, touching four tangible items, hearing three audible sounds, identifying two recognizable odors, and tasting one distinct flavor. Engage in exercises designed to redirect your focus to the present moment.

    b. Square Breathing: Inhale for a duration of four seconds, retain your breath for the same time frame, release your breath over four seconds, followed by a four-second rest. Repeat this cycle until you feel more composed.

• Break Tasks Into Smaller Steps

Break your study sessions and exam preparation into smaller, manageable tasks to prevent feeling overwhelmed. This can make your goals feel more attainable and reduce stress.

• Live in a Healthy Way

The combination of consuming a nutritious, balanced diet, leading an active lifestyle, and obtaining sufficient rest can enhance your overall well-being and enable you to cope more effectively with stress and anxiety.

• Seek Support

Approach friends, family, teachers, or counselors for guidance and support. Voicing your concerns and discussing your feelings can help mitigate stress.

• Develop a Test-Day Routine

Develop a routine for the day of the exam, incorporating relaxation techniques like deep breathing, progressive muscle relaxation, or meditation. This can help calm your nerves and place you in the correct mindset before the test.

• Practice Positive Self-Talk

Replace negative thoughts with positive affirmations and recall your preparation and capacity to succeed.

Here are a few instances of constructive self-dialogue:
- "I am well-prepared for this exam."
- "I can handle whatever comes my way."
- "I am capable of doing my best."

- **Accept Uncertainty**

Realize that it's not possible to know everything or anticipate every question on the exam. Concentrate on doing your best with the knowledge and skills you have honed during your preparation.

By adhering to these steps and suggestions, you can effectively manage stress and anxiety during your AP World History exam preparation and on the examination day, thus increasing your likelihood of attaining a high score.

Make the Most of Your Time During the Test

Efficient utilization of your time during the AP World History exam is crucial to ensure you can address all questions and deliver your best performance.

Here are more tips and examples on how to optimize your time during the test:

- **Familiarize Yourself With the Exam Format**

Prior to the test, familiarize yourself with the structure of the AP World History exam, including the number of sections, types of questions, and the time allocated for each section. Understanding what to anticipate will assist you in better managing your time on the day of the test.

- **Skim Through The Exam**

Take a moment when you get the test to quickly look over the whole thing. This will give you an idea of how the test is set up and help you figure out which questions may require more time or work.

- **Answer Easy Questions First**

Start by answering questions you are confident about or find easier. This will help you secure points early on and build momentum, leaving more time for challenging questions. For example, if you find multiple-choice questions easier, complete that section first before moving on to short answer or essay questions.

- **Use Time-Saving Strategies**

Employ strategies that can help you save time during the exam, such as:

- Underlining or circling keywords in the questions to help you focus on the most important information.
- Using shorthand or abbreviations when taking notes or outlining essay responses.
- Skipping questions you need clarification on and marking them to revisit later if time allows.

• Keep Track of Time

Regularly check the time throughout the exam to ensure you are on track—set milestones for completing specific sections to help you maintain a steady pace. For example, if the multiple-choice section has a 55-minute time limit, aim to complete half of the questions within the first 25-30 minutes.

• Allocate Extra Time for Essays

Essay questions often require more time due to planning, organizing, and writing your response. Be mindful of the time you spend on essay questions and allocate extra time accordingly. For example, if you have 90 minutes to complete three essay questions, allocate roughly 30 minutes per essay, but be prepared to adjust as needed.

• Use Outlining Techniques

Before writing your essay responses:

- Create a brief outline to help you organize your thoughts.
- Structure your response.
- Ensure you address all parts of the question.
- This will help you write more efficiently and stay on track.

• Keep an Eye on The Clock

While tackling the exam, periodically check the time to monitor your progress. This will help you decide if you need to accelerate or if you have spare time to devote to challenging questions.

• Review and Revise

If you complete the exam before time, use the remaining duration to revisit your answers, cross-verify your work, and make any necessary corrections. Be cautious not to overthink, as your initial instinct is often correct.

Remember that consistent effort, practice, and a positive mindset are key components of performing well in any exam. With diligent preparation and the right approach, you can confidently tackle the AP World History exam and excel in this challenging subject.

CONCLUSION

THE AP WORLD HISTORY STUDY GUIDE 2024 is a comprehensive and meticulously designed resource aimed at assisting you, the student, in successfully navigating the complex terrain of world history as you prepare for the AP exam. The book effectively covers a wide range of topics and themes, spanning from the earliest human civilizations to the most recent global developments. It employs various learning tools such as timelines, maps, charts, and illustrations to create an engaging and accessible study experience.

While this book conscientiously tackles a broad spectrum of topics, it's critical to recognize that no single reference can fully capture the depth and complexity of global history. As your study journey unfolds, you might come across certain unresolved issues or queries that surpass the capacity of this guidebook. To tackle these issues, you're urged to tap into additional resources like original documents, academic papers, and scholarly textbooks. These auxiliary materials can lend a more nuanced perspective of the topic at hand and contribute to cementing your understanding.

When gearing up for the AP exam, it's pivotal to bear in mind that triumph hinges on a solid groundwork in world history, coupled with honed critical thinking and analytical competencies. Achieving this entails proactive engagement with the study material, posing inquiries, and discerning interconnections across diverse epochs, regions, and themes. Beyond the pages of the AP World History Study Guide 2024, it is your responsibility to immerse yourself in the past's fascinating world.

To secure your achievement in the AP examination, here's your actionable plan: pledge a commitment to yourself to allocate sufficient time and energy towards your academic pursuits. Craft a methodical study blueprint that enables you to systematically examine the subject matter and focus on those aspects needing significant enhancement. Utilize the practice queries and test methodologies outlined in the book, and don't shy away from seeking advice from educators, classmates, and additional resources.

Lastly, as you continue on your academic journey, strive to develop a genuine curiosity and passion for history. Delving into history isn't simply about retaining dates, names, and incidents; it's about grasping the intricacies of human societies and the dynamics that have sculpted our world. The more knowledge you amass, the more equipped you'll be to comprehend the importance of historical occurrences and their connections to modern-day matters. By doing so, you foster a deeper sense of empathy, tolerance, and global cognizance — indispensable traits for any knowledgeable and participative citizen.

History is a repository of wisdom and enlightenment, and it's now your responsibility to decipher its enigmas and unearth its enduring teachings.

RESOURCES AND TOOLS

- *"Worlds Together, Worlds Apart: A History of the World from the Beginnings of Humankind to the Present" by Robert Tignor et al. (https://www.amazon.com/Worlds-Together-Apart-Beginnings-Humankind/dp/0393932087)*

- *"AP World History: Modern" by Princeton Review (https://www.amazon.com/Princeton-Review-World-History-Preparation/dp/0525570810)*

- *"Barron's AP World History: Modern" by John McCannon (https://www.amazon.com/AP-World-History-Premium-Practice/dp/1506253393)*

- *"Cracking the AP World History: Modern Exam" by The Princeton Review (https://www.amazon.com/Cracking-AP-World-History-Preparation/dp/0525568417)*

- *"Strive for a 5: Preparing for the AP World History Exam" by Robert W. Strayer & Eric W. Nelson (https://www.amazon.com/Strive-Ways-World-AP%C2%AE-Course/dp/1319186807)*

- *Khan Academy: World History Project - Origins to the Present (https://www.khanacademy.org/humanities/whp-origins)*

- *AP Classroom: AP World History: Modern (https://apcentral.collegeboard.org/courses/ap-world-history/classroom-resources)*

- *Quizlet - AP World History (https://quizlet.com/169735894/ap-world-history-flash-cards/)*

- *Reddit - r/APStudents (https://www.reddit.com/r/APStudents/comments/rsbui0/ap_world_history/)*

- *Crash Course World History on YouTube (https://www.youtube.com/playlist?list=PLBDA2E52FB1EF80C9)*

- *Fiveable's AP World History study resources (https://fiveable.me/ap-world)*

- *AP World History: Modern Course and Exam Description from College Board (https://apcentral.collegeboard.org/pdf/ap-world-history-modern-course-and-exam-description.pdf)*

Made in the USA
Las Vegas, NV
15 September 2023